An Introduction to the hudl 2

Jim Gatenby

BERNARD BABANI (publishing) LTD
The Grampians
Shepherds Bush Road
London W6 7NF
England

www.babanibooks.com

D1329067

Please Note

Although every care has been taken with the production of this book to ensure that all information is correct at the time of writing and that any projects, designs, modifications and/or programs, etc., contained herewith, operate in a correct and safe manner and also that any components specified are normally available in Great Britain, the Publishers and Author do not accept responsibility in any way for the failure (including fault in design) of any project, design, modification or program to work correctly or to cause damage to any equipment that it may be connected to or used in conjunction with, or in respect of any other damage or injury that may be so caused, nor do the Publishers accept responsibility in any way for the failure to obtain specified components.

Notice is also given that if equipment that is still under warranty is modified in any way or used or connected with home-built equipment then that warranty may be void.

This book is an independent publication and has not been endorsed by Tesco Stores Ltd.

© 2014 BERNARD BABANI (publishing) LTD

First Published – November 2014

British Library Cataloguing in Publication Data:

A catalogue record for this book is available from the British Library

ISBN 978-0-85934-751-8

Cover Design by Gregor Arthur

Printed and bound in Great Britain for Bernard Babani (publishing) Ltd

About this Book

The original Tesco hudl, referred to in this book as hudl 1, was an instant best seller. At £119 for a full-blown Android tablet, this success was hardly surprising. The hudl 1 has a very good technical specification and easy access to the Google Play Store, which now has over 1 million "apps" or software applications.

The hudl 2, launched in October 2014, has a bigger screen, faster processor, more memory and better sound and graphics. At £129 it's only half the price of some of its rivals. The hudl 2 has three excellent features not found on some tablets. These are a Micro SD card slot, GPS location technology and a Micro HDMI port for connecting the Hudl 2 to an HDMI TV or monitor.

The first chapter compares the hudl 2 with bigger computers and outlines applications of the hudl 2, such as news, entertainment, Web browsing and social networking. Setting up the hudl 2 and connecting to the Internet is discussed, followed by methods of operating the hudl 2, useful accessories and setting parental controls. Downloading apps from the Play Store and managing them on the Home and All Apps screens is also covered.

Browsing the Web using Google Chrome is discussed at length. eBooks, music, video, and live and catch up TV are then described, followed by e-mail, Skype and social networks. Using the hudl 2 as a Sat Nav is also discussed.

Taking photographs using the hudl 2's own cameras is described. Also importing photos from devices such as SD cards, Micro SD cards, USB devices and from smartphones using Bluetooth. Also the use of Dropbox and Google Drive "cloud" computing systems for storing files on the Internet and "syncing" files automatically to other computers. Printing from the hudl 2 to any printer using Google Cloud Print is also explained.

The hudl 2 and the hudl 1 are operated in virtually the same way. Any small differences are explained in the text.

About the Author

Jim Gatenby trained as a Chartered Mechanical Engineer and initially worked at Rolls-Royce Ltd using computers in the analysis of jet engine performance. He obtained a Master of Philosophy degree in Mathematical Education by research at Loughborough University of Technology and taught mathematics and computing for many years to students of all ages and abilities, in school and in adult education.

The author has written over forty books in the fields of educational computing, Microsoft Windows and more recently, tablet computers. His most recent books have included "An Introduction to the Nexus 7", which has been very well-received.

Trademarks

blinkbox Books, blinkbox Movies, blinkbox Music are trademarks or registered trademarks of blinkbox Entertainment Limited. hudl and hudl 2 are trademarks or registered trademarks of Tesco Stores Ltd. Google, Google Drive, Google Chrome, Gmail, Google Cloud Print, Google Maps and YouTube are trademarks or registered trademarks of Google, Inc. Microsoft Windows, Microsoft Word, Microsoft Publisher, Microsoft Excel and Skype are trademarks or registered trademarks of Microsoft Corporation. Facebook is a registered trade mark of Facebook, Inc. Twitter is a registered trademark of Twitter, Inc. Amazon Kindle is a trademark or registered trademark of Amazon.com, Inc. Dropbox is a trademark or registered trade mark of Dropbox, Inc. All other brand and product names used in this book are recognized as trademarks or registered trademarks, of their respective companies.

Acknowledgements

I would like to thank my wife Jill for her support during the preparation of this book and also Michael Babani for making the project possible.

Contents

3

Further Features

Entertainment

6

Browsing the Web   79

7

Communication and Social Networking   89

8

Working With Photos   **101**

9

Cloud Computing and File Management   **109**

Index   **117**

Essential Jargon

App

An application or program which a user runs, such as a game.

Operating System (O.S.)

The software used to control all aspects of the running of a computer. The hudl 2 uses the *Android 4.4 KitKat* O.S.

Processor

A chip executing millions of program instructions per second.

RAM (Random Access Memory)

The main memory, temporarily storing the current app.

Internal Storage

Permanent storage on which apps and files can be saved. The hudl 2 uses an SSD (Solid State Drive) with no moving parts.

Cloud Computing

Saving files on large *server computers* on the Internet, leaving more space on the Internal Storage of your own computer.

Syncing

Automatically copying and updating your files to the clouds, i.e. the Internet, so they are accessible to other computers.

Online

Connected to the Internet.

Screen Resolution

The number of dots or *pixels* in the screen. The hudl 2 has a resolution of 1920x1200, or about 300 dots per inch.

Streaming

This allows you to watch videos or listen to music *temporarily*, without saving a copy on your tablet's Internal Storage.

Downloading

A file is copied from the Internet and saved on your tablet. It can be accessed anytime in future, even if you are offline.

The hudl 2: An Overview

The Tablet Revolution

Hand-held tablet computers such as the Tesco hudl 2, the Google Nexus and the Apple iPad now meet a lot of the computing needs of many people. The hudl 2 is considerably cheaper than many of its competitors, while still providing a high level of performance. Despite its small size, the hudl 2 has real computing power, embracing the latest technology such as *voice recognition* and a *GPS* which really works. Apart from over a million *apps* for news and entertainment, the hudl 2 also includes excellent free software which saves and manages your *files* in the "clouds" on the Internet. Files include photos, pages of text and music, for example. So later you don't need to worry about where to retrieve them from. hudl 1 appeared in September 2013, with hudl 2 being launched in October 2014.

The Tesco hudl 2

The hudl 2 Really is a Powerful Computer

Tablets like the hudl 2 are actually more powerful than many of the desktop computers of a few years ago. This is confirmed by looking at the critical components which affect the performance of any computer. These are the *processor*, often referred to as the "brains" of the computer, and the *memory* or *RAM*, used to temporarily store the *app* or *program* currently being used, such as the Google Chrome Web browser. A *Solid State Drive (SSD)* is used as internal storage where apps and data files such as photos and documents can be permanently saved. The following table compares the hudl 2 with the original hudl 1. *Android O.S.* refers to the version of the operating system software which manages and controls the hudl 2 and hudl 1.

	hudl 2 (2014)	hudl 1 (2013)
Android O.S.	KitKat 4.4.2	Jelly Bean 4.2.2
Processor speed	1.83GHz	1.5GHz
Internal storage	16GB	16GB
External storage (Micro SD card)	Up to 32GB	Up to 32GB
Memory (RAM)	2GB	1GB
Screen resolution	1920x1200	1440x900
Screen size	8.3in	7in
Cameras (2)	Front facing (1.2MP) and rear facing (5MP)	Front facing (2MP) and rear facing (3MP)

Many laptop and desktop computers have inferior processor speeds and less RAM than the hudl 2 or hudl 1. Laptops and desktop computers do have much more internal storage, typically 500GB or more on a *hard disc drive*. However, tablets like the hudl 2 don't need this much internal storage, thanks to the use of *cloud computing* discussed on the next page.

How is this Small Size Possible?

How can a powerful computer be fitted into a small case like the hudl 2, when the main base units for some desktop computers are nearly as big as a suitcase? Here are some reasons:

Cloud Computing

The hudl 2 has no bulky hard disc drive — just a small, compact SSD, as mentioned on the previous page. The hudl 2 doesn't need a massive hard disc drive because all your documents, photos, etc., are automatically sent to the *clouds*. The clouds are actually *servers* or powerful Internet computer systems with high storage capacity. These include *Google Drive*, *Apple iCloud*, *Microsoft OneDrive* and *Dropbox* from Dropbox, Inc. You don't need to worry about where your documents are stored or how to retrieve them. You or your friends can access photos or documents, etc., stored in the clouds, from anywhere in the world, wherever you can connect a computer to the Internet.

Input and Output Ports

Laptop and desktop computers have lots of bulky ports for connecting monitors, mice, keyboards, etc., whereas the hudl 2 has only four tiny *ports* or sockets (as discussed shortly).

The hudl 2 has a built-in *touchscreen keyboard* which pops up when needed. Two tiny Dolby speakers, a microphone and two cameras are built into the hudl 2, so large ports are not needed. The hudl 2 has a *Micro USB* port into which the battery charger and other *USB* devices can be connected. The hudl 2 is powered by a small battery which lasts for about 8 hours between charges. A desktop computer requires a *Power Supply Unit* as big as a half a shoebox.

Downloading Music, Video and Software

Unlike laptop and desktop computers, there is no CD or DVD drive fitted to the hudl 2. Nowadays you can *download* and *stream* music, videos and software (apps) from the Internet to your computer — so you don't need a CD or DVD drive.

Tablet vs Laptop and Desktop Computers

There is currently much debate about whether the tablet will cause the demise of laptop and desktop computers. It really depends on what you want to do with a computer.

I use all three types of computer most days — tablet, laptop and desktop:

- To check the news, weather, look something up on Google, send a short e-mail, listen to music, watch TV or read the newspapers, the hudl 2 is ideal.

- To work for a session of several hours using DTP to typeset a book in my home office, I prefer my desktop computer with its 22-inch screen, large keyboard and mouse and plenty of work surfaces.

- To have the freedom to move to any room in the house to work on a long DTP document or a spreadsheet or edit and print a photograph, the laptop is the best choice.

For anyone who needs to use a computer on the move, etc., the hudl 2 is a good choice, being easier to carry than a laptop.

It has to be said that tablets in general are a bit small for producing long documents. I find the on-screen keyboard quite tricky to use when typing with the fingers but much better when used with a cheap *stylus*. (Like a pen with a soft tip.)

One solution in the future may be a *docking station* which converts a tablet, such as a hudl 2, into a desktop machine, with a separate keyboard, large monitor and a mouse. While away from home or the office, the hudl 2 is used as a touchscreen tablet. When you return to your base, the tablet is simply plugged into the docking station and used as a desktop machine.

A *Micro HDMI port* on the hudl 2 allows videos, etc., to be displayed on an HDMI TV or monitor. The hudl 2's *Micro USB port* allows USB devices such as a separate keyboard and a mouse to be connected to the hudl 2.

Typical Uses of the Tesco hudl 2

Listed below are some activities for which Android tablets such as the hudl 2 are well suited.

- Reading the latest news and weather forecasts.
- Reading online editions of newspapers and magazines.
- Reading electronic books using blinkbox Books, Google Books, or the Kindle app for the hudl 2.
- Listening to music and watching videos.
- Importing and viewing photographs.
- Watching live and catch up TV and radio.
- Searching the Web for information using Google and displaying Web pages using Google Chrome.
- Searching the Web using *spoken* questions.
- Looking at maps, including Google Maps, Google Earth and Google Street View.
- Using the hudl 2 as a Sat Nav, with Google Maps and the built-in GPS. Also using apps such as Navfree.
- Sending and receiving e-mails.
- Using social networks, such as Facebook and Twitter.
- Buying goods online and booking holidays and flights.
- Playing games such as Solitaire and Chess.
- Creating and editing text documents and small spreadsheets, including *speech recognition* text input.
- Tracking live flight information including aircraft location, speeds, altitude, bearing and ETA.
- Managing your online bank account and finances.
- Using *Skype* to make free, worldwide, voice and video calls between computers.

Keep Your Laptop or Desktop Computer?

As shown by the examples on the previous page, there's a huge range of activities possible with a tablet computer like the hudl 2. However, there are some tasks for which you really need a laptop or desktop machine. Fortunately, as the hudl 2 is relatively inexpensive, currently selling for £129, many people may be able to afford a hudl 2 as well as keeping a laptop or desktop machine.

The following tasks would be easier to accomplish on a desktop or laptop computer rather than on a tablet like the hudl 2.

- Typing a long document such as a letter, CV, report or student dissertation.
- Desktop publishing, including text and graphics, such as producing and editing a pamphlet, magazine or typesetting a book such as this one.
- Creating and editing a large spreadsheet, balance sheet for a business, personal accounts or large tables of text and figures.
- Design work such as architecture, graphic design, maps or engineering drawings (CAD).
- Creating, editing and updating Web sites.

The main problems with using a tablet for the above tasks are the small screen and keyboard. As mentioned elsewhere, there are various ways to increase the productivity of the hudl 2.

Connecting a hudl 2 to a Laptop or Desktop PC

As discussed later, you can connect a hudl 2 to a laptop or desktop PC using the USB cable provided with the hudl 2 for charging the battery. Then use the Windows Explorer or File Explorer on the PC to manage the files on the hudl 2, for tasks such as copying, moving, renaming and deleting files.

The Android Operating System

The *operating system* is a suite of programs or instructions which control every aspect of the computer's running. This differs from *applications* or *apps*, which are programs designed for a specific task, such as reading an e-book, editing a photograph or writing and sending an e-mail. Regardless of what app you are currently running, the operating system is constantly working in the background, controlling such functions as the screen display, saving documents or managing devices you've connected.

The Android operating system for the hudl 2 is produced by Google and widely used on tablets and smartphones. *hudl 2* currently uses the version of Android known as *KitKat 4.4.2*.

The Google Play Store

Over a million apps are available for standard Android tablets such as the hudl 2 and these can be downloaded from the Google Play Store, either free or costing just a few pounds, as described in Chapter 3.

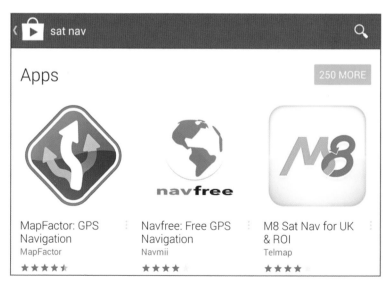

The Tesco Connection

The hudl 2 is a Tesco product but it's certainly not simply a marketing tool for the supermarket giant. In fact the hudl 1 was acclaimed as one of the best value tablets around and the much improved hudl 2 has therefore been extremely well received. Unlike some competing tablets, where the makers have 'tweaked' or modified the Android operating system, the hudl 2 uses the 'stock' or standard Android O.S., meaning it can easily access the Google Play Store with over 1 million apps.

The Tesco Apps

There are some Tesco specific apps you may wish to investigate, after tapping their icons on the Home screen or the all apps screen, as shown below.

Getting started shows you how to navigate around the hudl 2 and introduces some of the most popular apps.

blinkbox is part of Tesco. **blinkbox Movies** allows you to rent or buy the latest movies and TV shows for viewing on the hudl 2.

blinkbox Books gives you access to thousands of books which you can download and read on the hudl 2. Books can be saved on the hudl 2 for reading offline, i.e. where there is no Wi-Fi.

blinkbox Music is a free music streaming service, part of Tesco and supported by advertising. Millions of tracks are available from the major record companies.

The icon on the left appears at the top of the main Home screen, as shown below.

Tap the Tesco **T** icon shown above to display some of the latest Tesco news and information, as shown on the right.

Tap the icon shown here on the right and above right to display a range of Tesco online services. Tap any of these icons on the right to connect to a service, such as **Clubcard**, **Tesco Bank**, **Tesco direct**, **Groceries** and the **blinkbox** range, as shown in the small extract on the right.

However:

The Tesco shopping icons are quite unobtrusive and do not dominate the screens. You don't have to shop at Tesco to enjoy and benefit greatly from using the very versatile hudl 2.

Android Apps

Being a stock or standard Android tablet, the hudl 2 can use over a million apps from the Google Play Store for every conceivable purpose from games, music and entertainment, to health, fitness and lifestyle, for example.

Many apps are already installed on the hudl 2 when you buy it. Your apps are represented by icons on the All Apps screen, as shown below and on pages 11 and 12.

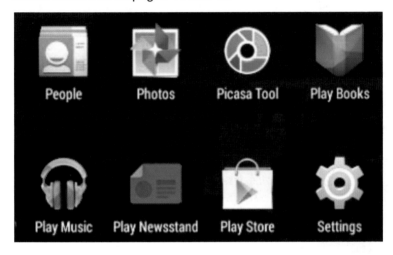

You can organize apps in *folders* representing different categories, such as Music, Games or Photography, for example. Icons can be moved around the Home screen as discussed in detail in Chapter 3.

The hudl 2 is operated using touchscreen gestures, such as *tapping* and *swiping*. For example, to launch Google, simply use your finger to tap the Google icon on the All Apps screen, shown on the next page. Touchscreen gestures are discussed in more detail in Chapter 2. As discussed later in this book, you can also use an inexpensive *stylus*, similar to a pen, or connect a separate physical keyboard and a mouse.

Some Popular Apps

The All Apps screen displays all the apps installed on the hudl 2, as shown in the small sample on page 10. Apps (applications or programs) are launched using a single tap on their icon with a finger or stylus. Listed below are some very popular and useful apps for the hudl 2, together with their icons.

Play Store

The **Play Store** icon gives access to over a million apps in different categories. These are either free or can be bought for a few pounds with a credit card. When a new app is installed its icon appears on the Home screen and on the Apps screen.

Google

Google is the world famous *search engine*. "To Google" means to search for information on a particular subject, after typing in some relevant *keywords*. The hudl 2 can also use *speech recognition* for entering the keywords.

Chrome

Google Chrome is a *Web browser*, similar to Microsoft's Internet Explorer and Apple's Safari. A Web browser is used to display Web pages and to move between pages using *links*. You can also revisit Web pages from your *browsing history* or which you have *bookmarked* for future viewing.

Gmail

Google mail or **Gmail** is a free and popular e-mail service allowing you to send and receive messages consisting of text, pictures and attached files. Creating a Gmail account and password gives you access to several other Google services.

Earth

Google Earth allows you to zoom in and view different parts of the Globe, using satellite images, aerial photography and images taken by cameras mounted on cars throughout the world. Google **Street View** in **Google Earth** shows 3D panoramic views of houses and buildings, etc., in a locality.

This icon launches either the front or rear camera on the hudl 2 to take ordinary photos, videos and "selfies". This is discussed in detail in Chapter 8.

YouTube is a free Google Website which allows individuals and companies to upload and share videos for other people to view. These may include amusing incidents or popular music videos, etc.

Skype allows you to make free Internet telephone calls between computers. The Skype app is free and the hudl 2 has the necessary built-in microphone, speakers and webcam. These enable free *video calls*, as well as voice calls, to be made to friends and family all over the world.

Facebook is the leading *social network*. Users post their *Profile* or *Timeline* on the Internet, make *friends* with people of similar interests, and exchange news, photos and videos, etc.

Twitter is a social network on which users post messages or *tweets* (up to 140 characters long). Celebrities may have thousands of followers reading their tweets. You can follow anyone, send replies to tweets or forward them to other people.

The hudl 2 can use **Google Books** or its own app, **blinkbox Books**, for reading e-books. You can also download the free **Kindle** app, the e-book reader from Amazon. There are millions of books and magazines to download cheaply.

2

Setting Up the hudl 2

Introduction

When you first take the hudl 2 out of the box, you may be as surprised as I was that such a small tablet, (also known as a *slate)*, can house a powerful computer. As discussed in Chapter 1, this is because a tablet doesn't need the bulky components like a hard drive, power supply unit, CD or DVD drive or sockets to accommodate cables for peripheral devices. Thanks to technical advances such as *cloud computing*, based on the Internet, these large components, normally found in laptop and desktop computers, are not needed in tablets.

Charging the Battery

Apart from the hudl 2 itself, the only other contents in the box are the battery charger and cable and some leaflets to get you started. (As mentioned on page 8, there is also a **Get started** app). Although the battery may be partially charged on delivery, the leaflet advises you to fully charge it for 3 hours before you get started. One end of the charging cable plugs into the *Micro USB port* on the side of the tablet, as shown on the next page. The other end of the cable has a full-size USB connector which can be inserted into a 3-pin 13-amp charger, (provided with the hudl 2). Alternatively the charging cable can be inserted into a USB port on a laptop or desktop computer. Charging via a laptop or desktop computer should be carried out with the hudl 2 in sleep mode or switched off. This method is slower than when the hudl 2 is connected to a charger plugged into a 13-amp socket.

A hudl 2 with a fully charged battery can be used for up to 8 hours before recharging is needed.

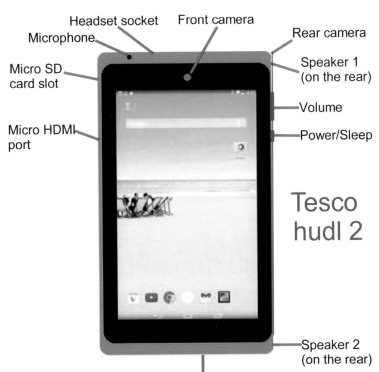

Microphone
Headset socket   Front camera

Micro SD
card slot

Micro HDMI
port

Rear camera

Speaker 1
(on the rear)

Volume

Power/Sleep

Tesco
hudl 2

Speaker 2
(on the rear)

Micro USB port, battery charger, etc.

Starting Up

Hold down the *Power/Sleep* key, shown above, until some colourful icons appear on the screen, followed by the word **hudl**. Then the *lock screen opens* as shown on the right. *Swipe* the padlock icon by touching it and sliding the finger across the screen. This opens the *Home* screen, discussed in the next chapter.

Connecting to Wi-Fi

In the home, this usually means connecting to a *broadband router*, normally included when you take out a contract with an Internet Service Provider such as BT, Virgin or Sky. Or it may mean connecting to the Wi-Fi provided in a hotel or café, etc.

After selecting your language, the hudl 2 should detect any available networks. Alternatively swipe down the screen and tap **SETTINGS** and **Wi-Fi** and set **Wi-Fi** as **ON**, as shown below. (You can also open **SETTINGS** by tapping its icon on the Apps screen, shown on the right.)

You should then see a list of networks available in your neighbourhood, such as **BTHub4-TFQ6** shown above.

Tap the name of the router or network you wish to connect to. The keyboard automatically pops up on the screen, enabling you to enter the password for the network, as shown on the next page. The password can usually be found on the back of a home network router. Otherwise, if necessary, the password should be available from the establishment providing the Wi-Fi, such as a hotel or café, etc. Tap **Connect** to complete the process of getting online to the Internet. The word **Connected** should now appear next to your selected router or Wi-Fi network, as shown on the right.

Checking Your Wi-Fi Connection

You can check your Wi-Fi settings at any time by swiping down from the top right-hand corner of the screen and tapping **SETTINGS** as shown in the **Quick Settings** panel below.

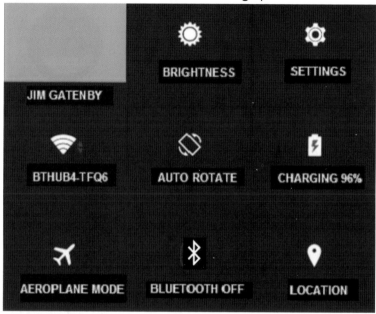

Then tap **Wi-Fi** to display your connection and any other available networks, as shown below

Creating a Gmail Account on the hudl 2

If you haven't got a Gmail account with an e-mail address and password, you can create one during the initial setting up process for a new hudl 2 tablet. It's worth opening a Gmail account because it gives access to several other free Google services, such as *Google Drive* cloud computing and *Google Docs* office software, as discussed in Chapters 1 and 9.

You can create a new Google account at any time by swiping down from the top right and selecting **SETTINGS**, as shown on the previous page. Then under **ACCOUNTS**, tap **+Add account**, then tap **Google** and **New**. You are then required to enter your first and last name and choose your e-mail address such as:

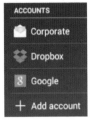

jimsmith@gmail.com

If your chosen name has already been taken you may need to choose a different name or add some numbers, such as :

jimsmith77@gmail.com

Creating a Gmail Account on a PC or Mac

You can also create a new Gmail account using a PC or Mac computer. Log on to **www.google.com** on the PC or Mac and select **SIGN UP**. Then enter your name, your new Google username (ending in **@gmail.com**) and password.

Syncing Files in the Clouds Using Google Drive

If you have a hudl 2 and a PC or Mac, for example, files such as photos saved in Google Drive on one machine are automatically copied or "synced" to all of your other computers, via the clouds, as discussed in Chapter 9.

Rotation of the Screen

The screen display can be locked in the vertical or horizontal position, similar to pictures in portrait or landscape mode. Alternatively the screen display can rotate automatically when you turn the tablet between vertical and horizontal positions. To change the rotation setting, swipe down from the top right of the

screen to display the **Quick Settings** panel, shown above. Then tap the centre button, which acts as a toggle switch between the **AUTO ROTATE** and **ROTATION LOCKED** settings.

Shutting Down

That completes the initial setting up of the hudl 2 and you should now be ready to start exploring the various screens and apps, as discussed in Chapter 3. As with any computer system, it's always a good idea to follow the recommended shutdown procedure — otherwise work may be lost if files are not closed before shutting down. Hold down the **Power/Sleep** key shown on page 14, until the following window appears. Then tap **Power off** as shown below, followed by tapping **OK** to finish shutting down.

Interacting with the hudl 2

The next few pages look at the ways we can interact with the hudl 2 and describe some useful but inexpensive accessories. The methods of operation are:

- Touch screen, the main method of using the hudl 2, including the on-screen keyboard, using fingers or *stylus*.
- External keyboard and mouse (connecting by Bluetooth, USB cable, or USB wireless dongle).
- Voice or speech recognition.

Touch Screen Gestures

- A single *tap* on an icon opens an app on the screen.
- Tap where you want to enter text and the *on-screen keyboard* pops up ready for you to start typing.
- *Swipe* or *slide* a finger across the screen quickly without hesitating, e.g., to scroll across the Home screens. Swiping also unlocks a locked screen and opens the Quick Settings panel. (Swipe down from the top right).
- *Touch and hold* an item such as an app or a widget, before dragging it to a new position with the finger.
- *Double tap* to zoom in or zoom out of a picture. In some apps *pinching* two fingers together or *stretching* apart can be used to zoom out or zoom in. This is useful, for example, to enlarge a Web Page in Google Chrome or make an area easier to see in the Google Maps app.

The Menu Button

On many screens, a menu button similar to the one shown on the right appears. Tap this icon to see a list of options relative to your current activity.

The On-Screen Keyboard

The touch screen method of controlling the computer works very well in most situations. The on-screen keyboard, shown below, pops up whenever you tap in a slot intended for the entry of text.

Hide the on-screen keyboard by tapping the icon shown on the right and on the Navigation Bar above.

The Stylus

If you find accurate typing difficult using the on-screen keyboard, a cheap *stylus*, (under £2) as shown on the right, may help.

Voice Recognition

When entering text in Google Search, the search bar displays a microphone icon, as shown below. Tap the microphone icon and then enter the text by speaking.

Google

Keyboard Options for the hudl 2

For general use you should find the on-screen keyboard quite adequate. However, for longer documents you might prefer to connect a separate physical keyboard.

There are 3 ways to attach a keyboard to a hudl 2. (A mouse can also be connected using the same technology.)

- A keyboard connected by USB cables to the Micro USB port on the side of the hudl 2, as shown on page 14.

- A wireless keyboard connected via a special USB dongle.

- A *Bluetooth* keyboard *paired* with the Bluetooth connectivity on the hudl 2.

Connecting a USB Keyboard

To use a keyboard which has an integral USB cable, all you need is a small extra USB cable, which converts the *Micro USB port* on the hudl 2 to a full-size standard USB port, as shown on page 105. These *OTG (On The Go)* cables are available from online retailers for under £2. Simply plug the Micro USB connector into the Micro USB port on the hudl 2 and connect the keyboard USB cable to the standard USB host end of the OTG cable. Full-size USB keyboards and mice can be bought for a few pounds. Several USB devices can be connected using a *USB hub*.

Connecting a Keyboard Using a Wireless Dongle

Wireless keyboards (and mice) are cheaply available. These use a *USB wireless dongle*, as shown on the right. The dongle plugs into the USB host connector on the OTG cable, as shown on page 105. No setting up is required — the keyboard should work straightaway.

USB wireless dongle

Connecting a Bluetooth Keyboard

Bluetooth is a type of wireless technology used for connecting devices such as keyboards, mice, etc., over short distances. To connect a Bluetooth keyboard to a hudl 2, swipe down from the top right and select **SETTINGS** then make sure **Bluetooth** is **ON**. Tap the word **Hudl 2** to display the words **Visible to all Bluetooth devices nearby**. With the Bluetooth keyboard switched on, tap **SEARCH FOR DEVICES** on the hudl 2. The Bluetooth keyboard should be detected by the hudl 2. Tap the name of the keyboard listed under **AVAILABLE DEVICES** on the hudl 2 to start *pairing* the hudl 2 and the Bluetooth keyboard. You may be asked to type a *PIN number* (provided on the hudl 2 screen) on the Bluetooth keyboard, then press **Enter** or **Return**.

The hudl 2 Micro HDMI Port

This allows the hudl 2 to be connected to an *HDMI* television or monitor, using an *HDMI to Micro HDMI* cable. Then you can use the big screen to watch videos, etc., running on the hudl 2. You can also attach a keyboard and mouse to the hudl 2, as discussed earlier, then use the big screen for word processing, etc. There's plenty of free office software available from the Play

HDMI to Micro HDMI

Store for the hudl 2, such as *Google Docs*, which includes word processing and spreadsheet apps, as discussed on page 113.

The hudl 2 Micro SD Card Slot

This allows a Micro SD card to be inserted in the hudl 2, increasing the storage from 16GB up to 48GB. By using an *SD card adapter* the Micro SD card can be used in a digital camera. Then the Micro SD card is removed from the camera and inserted into the hudl 2 for viewing or importing the photos. The Micro SD card slot is discussed in more detail on page 104.

Parental Controls

Parents can control their childrens' use of the hudl 2, as follows:

- Setting up a password, a PIN number or a pattern which must be entered to unlock the hudl 2 ready for use.
- Limiting the number of hours and times when children can use the hudl 2 both on weekdays and weekends.
- Blocking access to:

  certain categories of website.

  specific websites.

  specific apps.

To set up the hudl 2 for use by children, tap the **Child safety** icon shown below on the right. The apps below are some of the apps pre-installed on the Home screen of a new hudl 2.

After creating a profile with the child's name and age, you then set up the controls including time limits, preventing access to some Web sites and blocking the use of specific apps.

Exploring the hudl 2

The Home Screen

When you first start up the hudl 2 after holding down the Power /Sleep button, shown on page 14, you need to swipe the padlock icon on the Lock screen, also shown on page 14. The next screen you see is the *Home* screen, as shown on the right. In fact there are several panels on the Home screen which you can investigate by sliding or swiping horizontally in either direction. The Home screen is the starting point for your sessions on the hudl 2, from where you launch *apps* and *widgets*. The latter are small  windows which display information such as a calendar, a clock, the weather or a list of your e-mails.

A lot of apps are already installed by default on a new hudl 2 and you can add more from the Play Store. Icons for your favourite apps can be placed on a personal Home screen.

The *Navigation Bar* at the bottom of all the screens is shown below. The arrow on the left opens the previous screen. The house-shaped icon opens the central Home screen. The right-hand icon displays thumbnail images of recently opened apps.

The Favorites Tray or Hotseat

Along the bottom of the Home screen, as shown below, is the *Favorites Tray*, also known as the *Hotseat* on the hudl 2. This gives quick access to frequently-used apps. If you prefer, some of the default apps can be replaced by apps of your own choice.

The icons on the Favorites Tray above are as follows:

 This opens the **Google Play Store** of over one million apps.

 Tap to watch popular **YouTube** online videos.

 Google Chrome is the Web browser used on Android tablets like the hudl 2, as well as many laptop and desktop computers.

 This icon displays the **All Apps** screen shown on the next page. This is the only icon on the Favorites Tray which can't be replaced.

 Google Mail is an extremely popular e-mail service, discussed in more detail later in this book.

 The **Gallery** is used to store all the photos you take with the in-built cameras or photos imported from other sources, such as Micro SD cards, cameras, etc.

 As discussed in detail in Chapter 8, the **Camera** icon launches the built-in front and rear facing cameras.

The All Apps Screen

When you tap the All Apps icon on the Favorites Tray, shown on the right, the screen shown below appears, displaying many of the apps installed on the hudl 2. As discussed later in this chapter, you can find more new apps in the Play Store and install them.

Frequently-used apps can be copied from the All Apps screen to create a personal Home screen, as discussed shortly.

More Apps

From the All Apps screen, slide or swipe to the left to display a second apps screen. When you install new apps from the Play Store, their icons appear on this additional All Apps screen. As mentioned previously, you can move apps around, delete some of them and insert new ones, as discussed in detail shortly.

As shown above and on the All Apps screen on the previous page, there may be a lot of apps on your hudl 2 which you rarely use. You can tailor the Favorites Tray to include your most frequently used apps, as described on the next page.

Customising the Favorites Tray

The Favorites Tray on the Home screen on the hudl 2 is shown below. The All Apps icon shown on the right and below is fixed on the Favorites Tray and cannot be moved or deleted. The other icons on the Favorites Tray represent apps or *folders* and can be moved or deleted and replaced with apps which you use more frequently.

Removing an App from the Favorites Tray

Touch and hold the icon for the app you want to remove from the Favorites Tray. Hold your finger on the icon until an X in a circle appears at the top of the screen. Without lifting your finger, drag the icon over the X and drop it, deleting the app or folder. Removing an app from the Favorites Tray doesn't uninstall the app from the hudl 2. It's icon still appears on the All Apps screen. Alternatively, move an app from the Favorites Tray and slide it onto another part of the Home screen.

Moving an App to the Favorites Tray

Clear a space on the Favorites Tray by moving or removing an icon, as described above. To move an app on the Home screen to the Favorites Tray, hold your finger over the icon, then drag the icon to the space on the Favorites Tray. In the example below, the **Gmail** icon shown above (third from the right) has been removed and replaced by the **Photos** icon. The **YouTube** icon (second from the left above) has been replaced by the **Movies** *folder*. Folders are discussed on the next page.

Apps within Folders

The circular icon shown on the right represents a *folder* containing several apps. Folders can be created on the Home screens and also placed on the Favorites Tray. For example, you might want to create a folder for all your games or all your music apps. Or you could put the apps for **Facebook**, **Twitter** and **Skype**, shown below on the Home screen, in a folder called **Social**, for example.

Touch and drag the icons, one on top of the other, to form a single circular folder icon shown on the left below. Tap the folder icon to reveal the contents and to give a name to the folder if you wish. As shown below, tap **Unnamed Folder** and enter a name of your choice, **Social** in this example. Tap a circular folder icon to view and launch the individual apps within, as shown below.

To remove an icon from a folder, tap the folder, as shown on the left, to display the apps as shown in the middle above. Then briefly hold and slide the icon to remove it from the folder.

Customising Your Home Screen

When you start using a new hudl 2, the default setup may not be to your liking. In fact there are several panels making up the Home screen. These may already have default apps and *widgets* (discussed shortly) which you don't particularly want. You can tailor your Home screens in the following ways .

- Change the background colour or wallpaper.
- Delete any apps and widgets you don't want.
- Copy, from the All Apps screen, the apps that you want to use regularly and place them on your Home screen.

This will make a personal Home screen, showing just your most frequently-used apps and widgets, in addition to those on the Favorites Tray. To organise your apps further, you can group them in folders, as discussed on the previous page. Folders can be added to the Home screen and to the Favourites Tray.

(The apps placed on the Home screen are only copies, so removing them from the Home screen doesn't remove them from the All Apps screen or uninstall them completely.)

Changing the Wallpaper on Your Home Screen

Hold your finger on an empty part of the Home screen until the **WALLPAPERS** icon shown on the right appears.

Tap **WALLPAPERS** shown above on the right to display a selection of designs. Touch a design to select it.

Then tap **SET WALLPAPER** to apply the new background.

Deleting Apps from the Home Screen

You may have apps on the Home screen which you no longer use. Or you may think the default Home screen on a new hudl 2 is unnecessarily cluttered. You can safely remove apps and widgets from the Home screen. Tap and hold the unwanted app until a circled X appears at the top of the screen. Then drag the app over the X. As the apps (and widgets) on the Home screen are only *copies*, they are still available in the All Apps screen.

Unlike the Home screen, care should be taken with the All Apps screen, where it is possible to *uninstall* apps completely.

Adding Apps to Your Home Screen

To make up a personal Home screen with the apps you find most useful, open the Home screen where you want the apps to appear. Clear the screen of any apps and widgets you don't want. This is done by touching and holding the app or widget, then dragging onto the X, as described above.

Tap the All Apps icon as shown on the right then touch and hold the app you want to move to the Home screen. The Home screen opens. Keeping your finger on the app, slide it into the required position on the Home screen. A personal Home screen is shown below.

Widgets

Widgets appear alongside apps on the hudl 2 All Apps screen. However, unlike the icons for apps, a widget is a small window which displays information such as a calendar, your most recent e-mails, a clock or the weather, shown on the right. Tapping the widget, displays the information, such as a calendar, on the full screen.

Viewing Widgets

hudl 2

The **WIDGETS** tab on the hudl 1, shown at the bottom right of this page 1, is missing from the hudl 2. Instead you tap and hold an empty part of the Home screen until the **WIDGETS** icon appears, as shown below in the centre.

Tap the **WIDGETS** icon to see the widgets already installed on the hudl 2, such as the **Calendar** shown on the right. You can add further widgets from the Play Store, in the same way as apps, as described shortly.

hudl 1

The hudl 1 has a **WIDGETS** tab on the top left of the All Apps screen, as shown on the right, allowing you to display your widgets.

Creating a Widget Home Screen

The **Calendar** widget as displayed at the bottom of page 33 is not yet fully functional. You need to place a copy of a widget on an empty part of the Home screen before you can use it.

Although you can mix apps and widgets on the same Home screen, widgets tend to be much larger than apps and soon fill up the available space. So you may wish to put your most useful widgets on a separate Home screen panel.

Clear a Home screen panel by touching and holding any unwanted apps or widgets and dragging them onto the X, as shown on the right. Now open the **WIDGETS** screen as shown at the bottom of page 33. Touch and hold the required widget. Then slide the widget into the required position on the Home screen.

The Home screen below contains widgets for a digital clock and the local weather. Tap the widget to display it on the full screen.

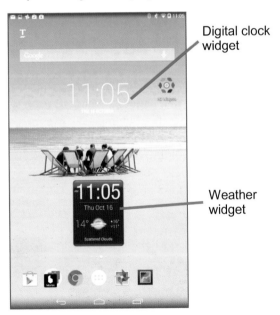

Digital clock widget

Weather widget

Resizing a Widget

Some widgets can be made bigger or smaller. Hold the widget for a few seconds and release your finger. If a rectangular frame appears with solid blue circles on each side, you can drag the circles to resize the widget.

Getting Apps and Widgets from the Play Store

The previous pages describe the way you can tailor your Home screen by sliding Apps and Widgets from the All Apps screen to an empty Home screen panel. A brand new hudl 2 has quite a lot of apps and widgets already installed by default on the All Apps screen. As discussed on page 33, the All Apps screen on the hudl 1 includes a **WIDGETS** section with its own tab. The widgets on the hudl 2 are displayed after tapping the **WIDGETS** icon, as discussed on page 33.

There are many more apps and widgets which can easily be downloaded from the Play Store. Many of these are free or can be purchased for a few pounds.

To open the Play Store, tap its icon shown on the right, on the All Apps screen or on your Home screen.

The Google Play Store

The Play Store has thousands of apps and widgets and various categories such as games, movies (to rent or buy), music, books and newspapers and magazines, as shown below.

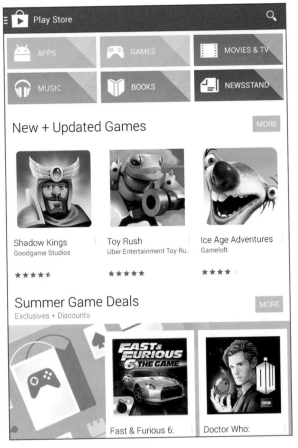

You can scroll through the various categories to find a particular item. Alternatively, you can carry out a search for an item such as an app, game, movie or book, etc., as discussed on the next page.

Searching the Play Store for Apps

As an example, a search will be made for an app for an on-screen music keyboard for the hudl 2.

First tap **APPS**, as shown on the main Play Store screen shown on the previous page. Then tap the magnifying glass search icon, as shown on the right.

Typing Keywords

The search bar appears as shown below, with a flashing cursor ready for you to type the name of the app or widget you wish to search for. The onscreen keyboard pops up automatically. Enter the keywords for the search, such as **music keyboard** and tap the search key (magnifying glass icon) on the keyboard.

Using the Microphone: Speech Recognition

Tap the microphone icon shown on the right. The small window shown below appears, requiring you to speak the keywords, such as **music keyboard**.

The speech recognition system on the hudl 2 is most impressive and immediately finds lots of music keyboard apps, as shown on the next page. You might like to practise searching for a few apps using the microphone. Apps I found in this way included **chess game**, **route planner** and **sound recorder**.

Downloading and Installing Apps

The search for music keyboards results in a long list of apps, as shown in the sample below. Most of these are free or at most cost only a few pounds.

To obtain an app, first tap its icon as shown above. If it's free of charge, the word **INSTALL** appears on the right. If there is a charge, the price is shown on the right, instead of **INSTALL**.

For a free app, tap **INSTALL** to download the app to the hudl 2. An icon for the app is placed on your All Apps screen and on your Home screen. The app should now be ready to open and use. If there is a charge for an app, tap the price and you will then need to buy it

by providing your bank details, before proceeding to install it.

Managing Your Apps and Widgets

Previous pages have shown how the new hudl 2 already has quite a lot of apps and widgets already installed by default on the All Apps screen. Some of these can be copied onto a Home screen tailored to your own requirements. The last few pages showed how you can obtain new apps and widgets from the Google Play Store and install them on your All Apps screen and on your Home screen.

Deleting Apps from the All Apps Screen

Care is needed if you try to delete apps or widgets from the All Apps screen. After touching and holding an app you previously installed, the word **Uninstall** appears at the top of the screen, next to a dustbin icon. If you slide the app over the dustbin icon or **Uninstall**, the app will be removed from the hudl 2. If you need the app again you'll need to reinstall it from the Play Store.

Default Apps or widgets are those already installed on the All Apps screens when the hudl 2 was purchased. These default apps and widgets do not have the **Uninstall** option when you touch and hold their icons in the All Apps screen. For example, if you try to remove default apps such as YouTube, Google+, Chrome, only **App info** is displayed on the All Apps screen.

Key Points: Apps and Widgets

- The hudl 2 is operated by tapping icons on the screen.

- Apps are small applications or programs such as a Web browser, a game or a drawing program.

- Widgets are small windows, usually displaying information such as a calendar, news or an e-mail inbox.

- The All Apps screen shows all of the apps and widgets installed.

- The Home screen consists of several panels which can be customized to display selected apps and widgets.

- Apps and widgets are copied from the All Apps screen by touching and holding, then sliding onto the Home screen.

- Further apps and widgets can be downloaded from the Google Play Store. New apps and widgets are placed on the All Apps screen and the Home screen automatically.

- At the bottom of every Home screen is a Favorites Tray which displays 7 icons for frequently used apps.

- The user can change 6 of the apps on the Favorites Tray.

- The Favorites Tray also displays the All Apps icon in the middle. The All Apps icon cannot be moved.

- Widgets cannot be placed on the Favorites Tray.

- Related apps can be grouped together and placed in folders, such as Social Networking, Photos, blinkbox, etc.

- Folder icons are circular, can have a name and can be placed on the Favorites Tray.

- Apps on the Home screen are only copies. Deleting them doesn't remove them from the All Apps screen.

- The Navigation Bar at the bottom of the Home screen has icons to return you to the Home screen and to display previously visited screens and app thumbnails.

Further Features

Introduction

This chapter looks at some more of the features built into the hudl 2 and, more precisely, its Android operating system. The features described in this chapter are:

Google Now and Google Cards

This feature provides Google searching for information using both voice and text queries. Google Cards automatically displays useful, real-time information for your current location.

Settings

Used to switch important settings on and off, make adjustments and tailor the hudl 2 to your own requirements.

Notifications

This screen keeps you up-to-date with new e-mail messages, calendar events, new downloads. Also Bluetooth, Wi-Fi, battery strength and aeroplane mode, as discussed shortly.

My Library

This is a widget that displays all the books, movies, music, etc., that are already on your hudl 2.

Calendar

Keeps track of all your appointments and sends reminders of imminent events, synchronised to your various devices.

Google Maps and Sat Nav

Displays maps of anywhere in the world, including Satellite and Street Views and Google Earth. Using the built-in Global Positioning System the hudl 2 can be used as a *Sat Nav*.

Google Now

This is an extension to the popular Google search engine. Google Now employs GPS (Global Positioning System) satellite technology to pinpoint your exact, current location. This is used to gather local information such as the weather and traffic conditions.

Google Now doesn't require any setting up. You just need to make sure **Google Now** is switched on in the **Settings**, together with **Location**, as discussed on page 47 and 48.

To open Google Now, swipe up from the bottom of the screen, or tap the Google icon on the All Apps screen, shown on the right. The Google Now screen opens with a search bar across the top, as shown below.

In the centre of the screen above is a *Google Card*. This is a small panel which pops up, unsolicited, to show current local information. Google Cards are discussed shortly.

Searching in Google Now

Typing Keywords

The search bar in Google Now shown below allows you to enter the keywords for a search, such as **weather in Florence**, by typing using the on-screen keyboard.

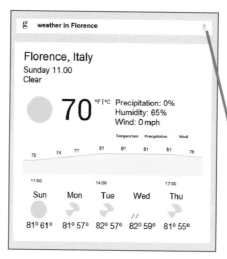

Spoken Queries

You can also tap the microphone icon, as shown above and on the right. Then speak your query into the hudl 2. Using spoken queries is discussed in more detail on page 37. The results of the search may produce a spoken answer, as well as a Google Card, as shown above. You will also see some traditional Google results as shown below, which you can tap to open Web pages relevant to your search.

Weather in Florence, Italy | 14 day weather outlook of Florence
www.worldweatheronline.com/Florence-weather/Toscana/IT.aspx

Latest **weather in Florence** Weather, Italy. Florence 14 day weather forecast, historical weather, weather map and Florence holiday weather forecast.

Weather Map - Florence, Italy weather - Monthly Averages

Perhaps you could experiment with a few spoken queries. For example, I said "tabby cat" with the microphone selected and received a spoken answer and a list of traditional Google search results with links to Web pages, as shown below.

Sporting Fixtures

If you enter or speak the name of a favourite sports team, such as Chelsea FC or Manchester United, Google Now gives the latest news and details of their next fixtures.

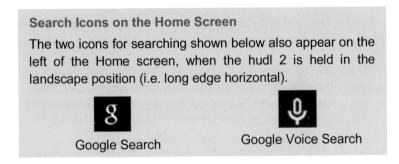

More on Google Cards

Google Cards pop up on the Google Now screen without you taking any action. For example, suppose you enquire about flights at your local airport, or about traffic on local roads. Google Now responds with Google Cards based on your recent activities. Google Cards are continually updated automatically, giving reminders of imminent events from you Calendar, fixtures for your favourite teams and news on topics you've been researching. You may also receive weather news based on your current location identified by the hudl 2's built-in *GPS* (*Global Positioning System* based on information from satellites).

After you swipe up from the bottom of the screen, Google Now display cards based on your previous activities and interests, such as the football results and share prices shown below.

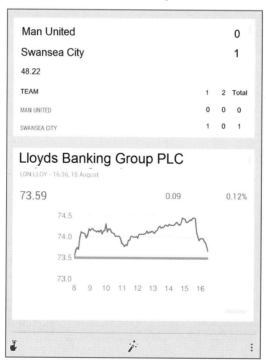

You can tailor Google Now to show updates, etc., using the icons at the bottom of the screen, shown below and on page 47.

 Use this icon to set **REMINDERS** to pop up on Google Now when a particular event is imminent.

 This allows you to select topics for which you wish to receive updates in Google Now, under the headings **Sports**, **Stocks**, **Places**, **TV & video**, etc.

 Tap this icon to open the **Settings** menu also discussed on page 47. This allows you to switch Google Now on and set various **SEARCH** and other options.

Flight Information

I recently made a Google enquiry about a flight from Frankfurt to Birmingham. Shortly afterwards a Google Card popped up with the latest flight information, as shown below.

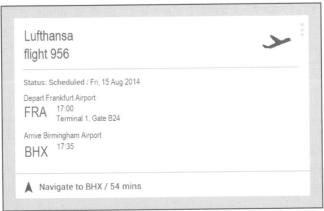

Tapping the blue message shown above and on the right turns the hudl 2 into a Sat Nav  based on Google Maps, with spoken directions to the destination, in this case BHX or Birmingham Airport.

Settings

In order to use Google Now, a number of features need to be switched on. These are probably already switched on by default, but you can easily check, as shown below. The main settings needed to fully use Google Now are:

- Google Now: **ON**
- Location: **ON**
- Location Mode: **High accuracy**

If **Google Now** is not **ON**, when you swipe up from the bottom, or tap the **Google** icon on the Home Screen, you only see the basic Google screen, not the more colourful **Google Now** screen, as shown on page 42. To turn **Google Now ON**, tap the menu icon shown on the right and below, at the bottom of the Google Now screen. (You may need to swipe slowly up from the bottom of the screen, dragging the Google cards upwards, to display the three icons shown below.)

From the menu which appears, tap **Settings** and then make sure **Google Now** is **ON** as shown below, by tapping **OFF** on the right, if necessary, then tapping **YES, I'M IN**.

Switching Location (GPS, etc.) ON

hudl 2

Swipe down from the top right of the screen, to display the **Quick Settings** panel shown at the top of page 49. Then select **SETTINGS** and under **PERSONAL** tap **Location**, as shown below.

If necessary tap on the top right to make sure **Location** is **ON**, as shown below.

Tap **Mode** shown above and you see that **High accuracy** uses **GPS**, **Wi-Fi** and **mobile networks** to determine your location.

hudl 1

In **SETTINGS** tap **Location access** and make sure the three settings below are **ON** and ticked respectively.

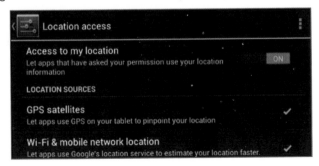

Quick Settings

Swipe down from the top right of the screen, to display the **Quick Settings** panel, as shown below.

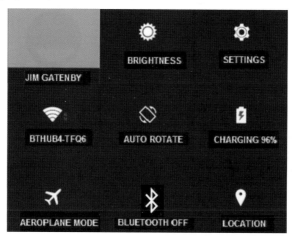

Tapping **BTHUB4-TFQ6** (in this example), allows you to check your Wi-Fi connection, as discussed in Chapter 2. **AUTO ROTATE** keeps the screen upright when the hudl 2 is turned on its side. The alternative setting, **ROTATION LOCKED**, keeps the screen display in a fixed position relative to the hudl 2's casing.

BLUETOOTH allows devices such as keyboards to be connected wirelessly to the hudl 2, as discussed on pages 23 and 108.

AEROPLANE MODE switches off the hudl 2's Internet connection, for flight safety. The hudl 2 can still be used *offline*.

LOCATION is used to switch on **GPS**, pinpointing your current position and allowing you to plan routes using Google Maps.

The **SETTINGS** icons shown above and below open the full **Settings** screen, shown on the next page.

hudl 2

hudl 1

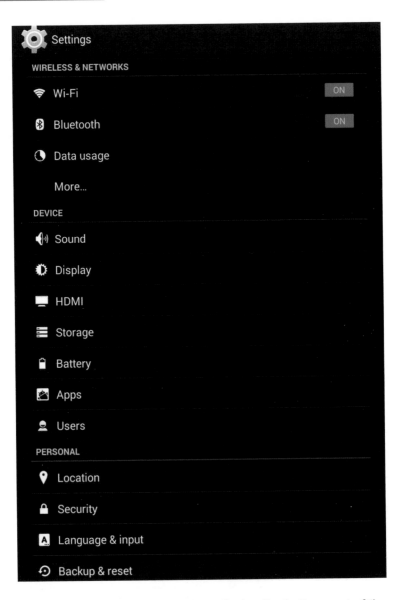

It's necessary to swipe upwards to display the bottom part of the **SETTINGS** menu, as shown on the next page.

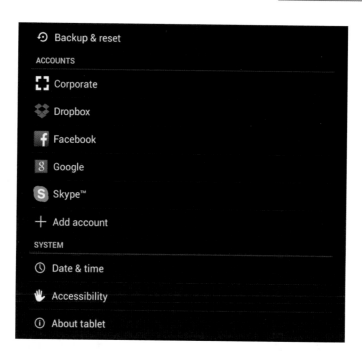

The **Settings** menu allows you to check your Wi-Fi and any Bluetooth connections. You can alter the screen brightness and wallpaper and the sounds emitted when various events occur. **Apps** on the previous page lists all your applications and gives you the chance to disable them. **Users** lists the people who can use the hudl 2 and allows the addition of profile information.

Location is where you can make sure **GPS** is active, so that you can access local information as discussed on page 48. **Security** includes the setting of a password to unlock the hudl 2. You can also limit the installing of apps to those from the Play Store and disallow apps from other sources. Apps in the Play Store have been thoroughly checked for malicious software.

Other settings include the creation of accounts on Skype, Dropbox and Google, etc. **Accessibility** provides help for those with special needs such as poor eyesight, etc.

Notifications

Across the top of the Home and All Apps screens there are two groups of very small icons.

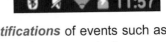

The group on the left above are *notifications* of events such as receiving an e-mail, capturing a screenshot or events from your calendar. The group of small icons on the right above are *system icons*. The icons in this group change according to your settings. For example, icons may be present which show Bluetooth ON, sound OFF, aeroplane mode ON, Wi-Fi ON, the battery state of charge and the current time.

To display your notifications more fully, as shown in the example below, swipe down from the top left of the screen. If a notification refers to an e-mail, tap to read the message. Once you've looked at a notification, it's removed from the list.

Tapping the icon, shown on the right and at the top right below, dismisses all notifications.

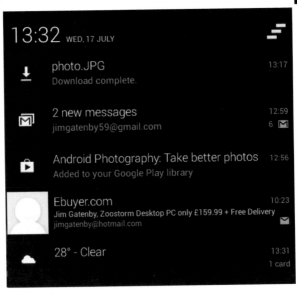

My Library

This is a widget that displays all the music, magazines, books, and movies that are installed on a hudl 2. Some of these media may be already installed from new or you may have added more from the Google Play Store.

The **My Library** widget may already be displayed on one of your Home screens. If not, open the **Widgets** screen as described on page 33 and scroll across until you see the **Play – My Library** widget as shown on the right. Touch and hold this widget, then slide into a convenient place on the Home Screen. The **Play – My Library** window opens as shown below on the right to display icons for all of your installed media **My music**, **My books**, **My newsstand**, **My music & TV**. Tap a thumbnail, e.g. of a book cover as shown in **My books** on the bottom right, to read the book, listen to music or watch a movie, for example.

To make room for **My Library**, widgets and apps which you no longer need can be deleted by holding and sliding over the circled X at the top of the screen. (Removing an app or widget from the Home screen doesn't totally remove it — the app or widget will still be present on the All Apps screen).

The Google Calendar

The Calendar on the hudl 2 has many useful features including the following:

- Keeping a record of all your future events.
- Sending you notifications of imminent events.
- Synchronizing changes between various devices, such as your hudl 2, smartphone, laptop or desktop PC or Mac.

The Calendar on the hudl 2 can be opened by tapping its icon on the All Apps screen, as shown on the right.

The Calendar opens as shown in the example on the right, displaying the events for the current week. An arrow at the top, next to **Week**, opens a menu enabling you to display **Day**, **Week**, **Month** or an **Agenda** listing all of your events. When a **Day** or a **Week** are displayed, the current month is also displayed at the bottom left, as shown on the right. You can scroll through displays of the days or weeks by swiping horizontally. To scroll through the months swipe vertically.

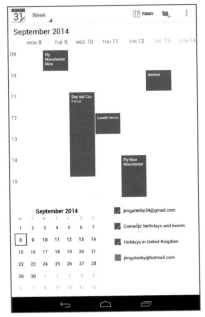

Creating a New Event or Editing an Event

Tap the **New event** icon, shown on the right, at the top of the calendar or tap twice in the correct hourly slot on the appropriate day. To edit an existing event tap the pencil icon. Now enter or amend the details of the event such as the time and place.

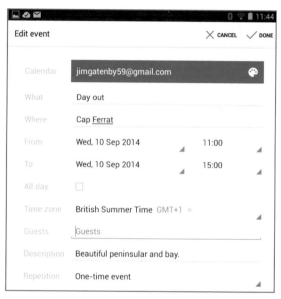

At the bottom of the **New event** or **Edit event** screen you can set a **Reminder** in the form of a notification or an e-mail. With a notification there is a beep and then an event, such as **Barbecue** in this example, appears in the **Notifications** panel, as discussed on page 52. Tap the event name for further details, as shown below.

The Calendar Widget

A Calendar widget appears in the WIDGETS screen. This can be placed on a suitable clear space on the Home screen. This is done by touching and holding the widget and then sliding into position on the Home screen, as described in more detail on page 33. The Calendar widget lists all your forthcoming events, automatically updated with information from the Calendar app.

Calendar widget

Tap the Calendar widget to open the Calendar app full screen for editing existing entries or adding new events.

Syncing Your hudl 2 Calendar with a PC, etc.

The Google Calendar can be viewed on all the common platforms — hudl 2, Nexus, iPad, laptop or desktop PC or Mac, etc. On a PC or Mac open **www.google.co.uk**. If necessary **Sign in** with your Gmail address (or **Sign up** for a new one). Then select the **Apps** icon on the top right of the screen, shown here on the right. From the drop-down window which appears, select the **Calendar** icon, shown below, to open the Calendar.

New events can be added to the Calendar on any of your devices. Any changes to the Calendar are automatically synced across to all the devices you sign in to.

Google Maps

The hudl 2 has an icon for Google Maps already installed on the All Apps screen, as shown on the right. When you first tap the **Maps** icon, it opens to show a map of your current area. To find a map of another area, enter a *place name* or *post code* in
the search bar. In this example, **Farne Islands** was entered. Stretch or pinch the map with two fingers to zoom in or zoom out.

Tap the menu icon at the top left of the screen, shown below, to see a menu of alternative views of the area, i.e. **Satellite**, **Terrain** and **Google Earth**, as shown on the right below.

Terrain is the basic map view shown above on the right. Both **Satellite** and **Google Earth** display satellite images of the area. **Google Earth**
has another menu, shown below on the left, allowing you to display additional information, such as businesses, places of interest, etc., as shown in the example on the right below.

Bamburgh Castle

Bamburgh Castle is an imposing castle located on the coast at Bamburgh in Northumberland,

Using the hudl 2 and Google Maps as a Sat Nav

The built-in *GPS* in the Hudl 2 is used for identifying your precise location when planning a journey and also en route. Make sure **Location/GPS** is switched **ON**, as shown on pages 47 and 48. The hudl 2 is Wi-Fi only, so set up a route *before* setting off, i.e. while still connected to the Internet.

In Google Maps, enter the name or post code of your destination. Google Maps responds with the travelling time from your current location to your destination, with details of roadworks and traffic.

Tap the time (e.g. **4hr 23min** shown below) and if necessary select your mode of transport. A map of the route is displayed.

If necessary, there is an option to view and select an alternative route, as shown on the left below. Tap the time to display a listing for the route and scroll if necessary to see the whole list.

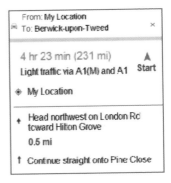

When you're ready to set off, tap the **Start** arrow shown on the right and above right to start receiving spoken directions for each stage of your journey.

There are several other Sat Nav apps available in the Google Play Store discussed in Chapter 3, such as Navfree and CoPilot.

Using a hand-held device while driving is illegal. A mounting bracket makes the hudl 2 *hands-free*, but you may still be prosecuted if you're thought to be distracted by the Sat Nav.

Entertainment

Introduction

Amongst many other things, the hudl 2 is a versatile entertainment platform. The following activities are discussed in this chapter:

- eBooks — electronic books which may be downloaded from the Internet for reading offline at any time.

- Music, magazines, movies and games downloaded free or bought or rented.

- YouTube — a Google-owned Web site enabling you to play free music and videos uploaded by other people.

- Live and catchup TV and radio.

The small size of the hudl 2 means you can use it anywhere — on a sofa, in bed or in a public place such as a hotel. You can stow it in a bag and take it on holiday; many places such as hotels and restaurants now have free Wi-Fi so while you're away you can still go online for all your favourite Internet activities. The hudl 2 may also be used for your personal in-flight entertainment, if your airline allows it. At the time of writing *Aeroplane mode* or *flight mode* must be switched on to prevent possible interference with the aircraft's instruments. Flight mode was discussed on page 49 and only allows you to use the hudl 2 *offline*, i.e. not connected to the Internet. Such offline activities would include reading an e-Book or watching movies saved for offline use, before boarding the aircraft.

eBooks

Many 20th century projects involved devices for reading books electronically on a screen. The Amazon Kindle, introduced in 2007, quickly became a best-seller, being extremely light and affordable and an efficient alternative to the book printed on paper. A tablet like the hudl 2 allows you to save lots of books on its internal storage, making it easy to take a selection of books with you on holiday, for example.

There are several apps for using the hudl 2 as an eBook reader:

blinkbox Books

blinkbox (rather than Blinkbox) is part of Tesco and the *blinkbox Books* app is pre-installed on the hudl 2. It can also be used on other platforms such as the iPad. blinkbox Books gives access to hundreds of thousands of e-books for downloading to your hudl 2.

Google Play Books

The hudl 2 uses the standard or stock Google Android operating system, so it's fully compatible with the Google *Play Books* app, enabling you to download and read titles from the millions of books in the Play Store. The Play Books app should be pre-installed on the hudl 2 — if not it can easily be downloaded from the Play Store, as discussed on page 38.

1. Google Play Books
Google Inc.
★★★★

The Kindle eBook Reader App

The Kindle app can be downloaded from the Google Play Store and installed on the hudl 2. Millions of books are then available from the Amazon Kindle Store. You need to sign up for an Amazon account.

1. Kindle
★★★★

Using blinkbox Books

When you first tap the **blinkbox Books** icon shown on the previous page, you are required to register with your e-mail address, name and a password. You can also enter your Tesco Clubcard number if you want to earn points from purchases.

The opening screen displays some covers of books which you might like to sample. The **Options** button below each book allows you to see the book's contents and to read a sample, as well as an option for buying the full book.

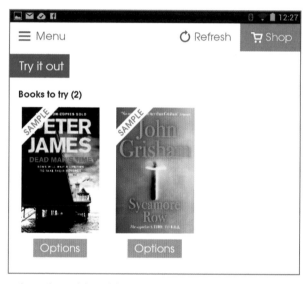

After you've signed in with your e-mail address and password, tap **Shop** at the top right of the screen to start searching the full catalogue of **blinkbox Books**, as shown on the next page.

Finding Books

At the top of the **Shop** screen is a search bar, allowing you to look for a book title or author you are interested in.

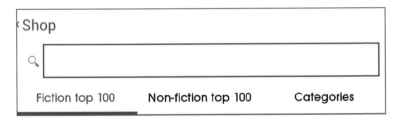

As shown above, you can also display the top 100 non-fiction and fiction titles. The **Categories** option shown above allows the books to be displayed under various headings such as **Biography & Memoir** shown below.

There are many other book categories, including **Food & Drink**, **History**, **Humour**, **Romance** and **Travel & Holiday**.

After you've selected a category or top 100, etc., the covers of the books are displayed with the prices, as shown in the small sample below. A similar screen would appear if you entered the name of a well-known author in the search bar, shown near the top of the previous page.

Reading a Sample

If you tap the cover of a book, you can read a description of the book and the author, view the contents and read some sample pages, as shown on the right. blinkbox have made 10% of every book available to be read as a free sample. If you want to be able to read the sample offline, i.e. where there is no Internet or Wi-Fi, tap **Save sample**, to store a copy of the sample on the internal storage of your hudl 2.

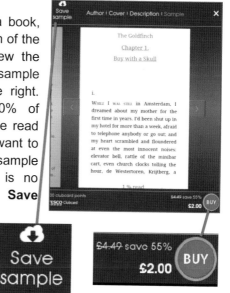

Buying a Book

If you decide to buy the book, tap **BUY** at the bottom right of the screen, as shown on the right and at the bottom of the previous page. You are asked to enter and confirm your password every thirty minutes. Then you are asked to add a new credit card to the account associated with your e-mail address. This will allow you to buy books and download and save them to your hudl 2 so you can read them offline. This is useful, say, if you want to take books to read on holiday in a place where there is no Wi-Fi. Or on a flight where you are usually asked to set your tablet in Flight Mode or Aeroplane Mode, i.e. with no connection to the Internet.

Downloading a Book for Reading Offline

When you buy a book, it's saved in **Your Library** in the clouds, i.e. on the Internet. At this stage the book is not saved on the internal storage of your hudl 2.

When you tap **Menu** you can select **In your cloud** to display the books you've bought.

Tap the cover of a book to download a copy and save it on your device, i.e. on the internal storage of the hudl 2.

If you tap **Menu** again, you should see that **On your device** is now highlighted, as shown below. **In your cloud**, previously highlighted, is now in a faint grey or "greyed out", meaning the option is not currently available.

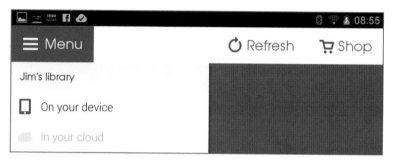

Removing a Book from the hudl 2

Tap **On your device**, as shown above, then tap **Options** under the image of the book cover, as shown on the right.

Then tap **Remove book from your device** from the menu which appears, as shown below.

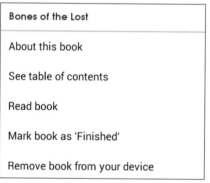

Removing a book from your device, i.e. your hudl 2, does not remove it from your library. The book will still be available if you want to download it again at some time in the future.

Reading an eBook in blinkbox Books

After you've downloaded a book, as described on page 64, tap the book cover again to open it for reading, as shown on the right. To move forward or back through the pages of the book tap in the left or right margins or swipe across the screen from the left or right.

Tap in the centre of the screen to bring up the screen shown on the lower right. This shows the name of the author, a button to Bookmark a page and a button for the **Options** menu. Along the bottom of the screen is a bar showing how far you have progressed in reading the book.

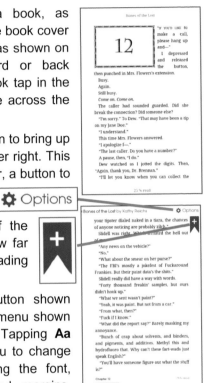

If you tap the **Options** button shown above and on the right, the menu shown on the left below appears. Tapping **Aa Reading settings** allows you to change the text formatting, including the font, brightness, line spacing and margins, etc., as shown on the right below.

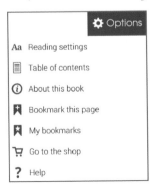

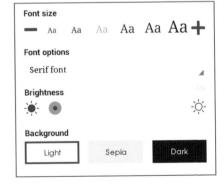

Google Play Books

As mentioned on page 60, the hudl 2 is a stock Android tablet, so it can access apps and resources in the Google Play Store including millions of books, as discussed on page 36. The Play Books app should be installed by default on the hudl 2, but if necessary can be installed from the Play Store as described on page 36.

Tap the Play Books icon as shown above on the right then tap **Read now** or **My Library** (whichever is shown on the top left of the screen) to display the menu shown on the right, which includes the **Shop** option.

Tap **Shop** to open the Play Store. The books are displayed in various categories, similar to the Shop

described in the previous section on blinkbox Books. Tapping the small three dot menu button below the image of the book cover gives options to buy the book or read a free sample. After you've bought a book using your credit card, etc., the book is stored in your library, as before with blinkbox Books.

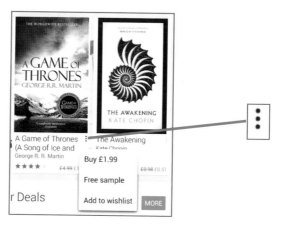

Downloading a Book Using Google Play Books

If you want to download a book in Google Play Books, select **My Library** as shown below.

Book saved
in clouds only

Book saved
in clouds and
on the hudl 2

Initially a book is saved only in **My Library** in the clouds, denoted by a dark angled pin, as shown above on the left. Tap this icon to download the book to your hudl 2. A book which has been successfully downloaded and saved on the hudl 2 displays a white vertical pin, as shown on the right above.

Deleting a Book in Play Books

With the book displayed in My Library in Play Books, tap the three dot menu button below the book cover, shown on page 67. **Don't keep** removes the book from the internal storage of your tablet — so you won't be able to read it unless you have Wi-Fi or an Internet connection. **Delete from library** removes the book from your library in the clouds.

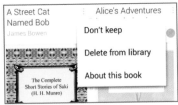

The Kindle App for the hudl 2

To read eBooks in the popular Kindle format, it's just a case of installing the Kindle app from the Google Play Store. Tap the Play Store shopping bag icon, shown on

the right and on the right of the Favorites Tray. Then tap **APPS** and tap the magnifying glass search icon. Type **Kindle** into the search bar or tap the microphone icon and say **Kindle** to display a list of Kindle apps, as shown in the sample above.

Tap the Amazon Kindle app shown on the left above and tap **INSTALL** to put an icon, shown on the right, on your All Apps and Home Screens. Sign in with an e-mail address and password for an Amazon account or create a new account.

To start reading one of the Kindle books you already have, tap the front cover.

Tap **Store** at the top right of the screen to open the Amazon Book Store of over 2 million books. If you have an account with Amazon, you can buy books very easily using **Buy Now with 1-Click**.

eBook Readers in General

The apps for blinkbox Books, Google Play Books and the Amazon Kindle use similar methods for reading eBooks, i.e. swiping or tapping left or right to turn pages and tapping in the centre of the screen to open formatting tools, bookmarks, etc.

Music on the hudl 2

blinkbox Music

An icon for the **blinkbox Music** app, as shown on the right, is pre-installed from new on the hudl 2.

blinkbox Music is a free *music streaming* service, with advertising, owned by Tesco and with access to over 12 million tracks and nearly a million users.

Features of blinkbox Music

- Radio stations/playlists created by blinkbox Music resident DJs and also celebrities.

- Playlists already created for special occasions.

- Search for artists or types of music and blinkbox Music creates a station including similar music.

- Create your own **Favourite Station** playlist based on your favourite tracks.

- Download and save stations on the hudl 2 for listening offline, when you have no connection to the Internet.

- Share stations with friends using e-mail and social networks such as Facebook and Twitter.

After you tap the **blinkbox Music** icon shown above, the main **Browse Stations** window appears, as shown in the small extract below. Tap a station to sample the music.

The Menu Button

At the right of each station is the commonly used, 3 dot menu button, shown on the right and below.

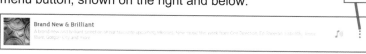

Brand New & Brilliant

Use this menu to **Start** playing a station, or tap **Favourite this Station** if you want to keep this station. Tap **Download this Station** to save the station for playing offline.

Share this Station allows you to send the station with an e-mail or post it on Facebook or Twitter.

- ⊙ Start this Station
- ☆ Favourite this Station
- ⤓ Download this Station
- ⪪ Share this Station

 Tap the menu icon shown on the left, at the top left of the **Browse Stations** window. This displays the menu shown on the right. **Browse Stations** opens the window shown at the bottom of the previous page. **Find a Station** presents a search bar into which you can enter the name of an artist or a type of music, etc. Then blinkbox produces a list of

▮ blinkbox Music

((•)) Browse Stations

◯ Find a Station

♪ My Station

☆ Favourite Stations

⤓ Downloaded Stations

relevant stations. **My Station** plays the music you've "liked" or similar and avoids the music you've disliked, using the icons shown on the right. These icons appear at the bottom of the **Browse Stations** window. **Favourite Stations** above lists the stations you've marked as favourite, using the menu shown at the top of this page.

Downloaded Stations are those saved on the Hudl 2's internal storage for playing offline.

Google Play Music

The hudl 2 can use the vast choice of music in the Google **Play Store**. An icon for the Google **Play Music** app is pre-installed, as shown on the right. Tap this icon, then tap in the top left-hand corner of the screen and select **Shop** and tap to open the **Music** section of the Play Store. Then browse for some music, using the various **GENRES**, such as **Classical**, or **Pop**, etc.

Alternatively tap the search icon, then enter the name of the record or artist or tap the microphone icon and speak the words.

Tap the cover to buy a single or album. Also shown is the familiar three dot menu which, in this example, has options to **Add to wishlist** or **Buy £0.99**. After buying a piece of music it's added to your library in the clouds.

A track or album can be played after tapping the **Play Music** icon shown at the top right of this page.

Tap in the top left-hand corner of the screen to make sure **Listen Now** is displayed. Then tap the three dot menu icon on the front cover, shown on the right, to display a list of options, including **Download**, i.e. save the track or album on the hudl 2.

If the music has been downloaded and saved previously, **Remove download** is displayed on the menu. This deletes the track or album from the hudl 2, but not from your library.

Movies and TV

blinkbox Movies

blinkbox Movies (rather than Blinkbox) is a movie and TV streaming service owned by Tesco. The movie and TV service was the first of the blinkbox brand, which has recently been expanded to include *blinkbox Books* and *blinkbox Music*, described earlier in this chapter.

Features of blinkbox Movies

- Select from a choice of 20,000 movies and TV shows in various categories.

- You can choose to rent or buy.

- There is no monthly subscription.

- Your payments earn Tesco Clubcard points.

- blinkbox is generally used for *streaming* rather than *downloading* movies and TV shows.

- If necessary you can continue watching movies and TV shows on blinkbox on other types of computer.

Signing Up for blinkbox Movies

The blinkbox Movies app is pre-installed on the hudl 2 as shown at the top right of this page. After tapping the icon, you can either **Sign in** or **Sign up** with an e-mail address and password, different from those used in blinkbox books or blinkbox music.

Once you've signed up you can choose from **Movies** or **TV** in various categories such as **Best Selling** or **Top Rated** and various genres such as **Comedy**, **Action**, **Drama**, **Thriller**, etc., as shown on the right and on the next page.

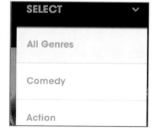

Tap on a movie or TV show you want to watch and then tap **WATCH NOW** and choose if you want to **RENT** or **BUY**.

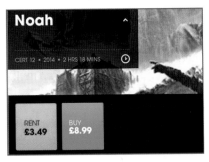

If you **RENT** a movie or show, you have 30 days to start watching it and then 48 hours in which to complete the viewing.

Connecting the hudl 2 to a Big Screen

The hudl 2 has a *Micro HDMI port*, as shown on page 14 and discussed on page 23. This allows you watch your hudl 2 movies, etc., on an HDMI TV or monitor. All you need is an inexpensive cable connecting the Micro HDMI port on the hudl 2 to an HDMI port on a TV or monitor.

Google Play Movies & TV

The Play Store contains a range of movies and TV shows in various categories, etc., as shown below.

Some can be bought or rented while others can only be rented. You may have to begin watching a movie within 30 days of renting it and the rental may expire 48 hours after you start watching it.

Tap **RENT** or **BUY** then select **PLAY** or **DOWNLOAD**.

To watch a movie you've bought or rented, tap the **Play Movies & TV** icon shown on the right, which appears on the Apps screen, then tap **PLAY**.

Downloading for Offline Viewing – the Pin Icon

To make a movie watchable offline, tap the angled pin icon on the movie graphic, shown on the right. This starts downloading the movie. The pin icon starts to fill with colour and, when completely full, the download is complete. The pin icon is now white and vertical, as shown on the right. A notification should also be displayed when you swipe down from the top left-hand corner of the screen, as discussed on page 52.

YouTube

The movies and TV apps discussed on the previous pages allow you to buy or rent commercial films. In contrast, YouTube is a Web site, owned by Google, which provides a platform for ordinary people to share videos which they've recorded themselves. These can rapidly become very popular and "go viral" when millions of people watch them around the world.

To launch YouTube, tap the icon shown on the right. The YouTube screen shows a long list of video clips which can be scrolled up and down by swiping. Swipe from left to right to display the menu shown below. To watch a video, tap a menu option such as **Popular on YouTube** or **Sport** and, if necessary, scroll vertically to display the cover picture and title of the required video. Tap the picture to start the video. To pause a video, tap the screen and then tap the pause button.

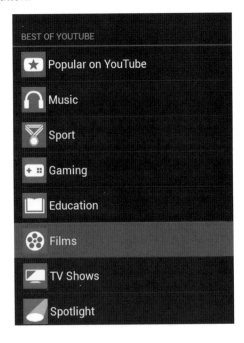

Live and Catchup Television and Radio

The Google Play Store includes the free BBC iPlayer app, as shown on the right. This can be obtained from the Play Store and installed on your hudl 2 using the methods described on pages 36-39. Tap the icon shown on the right to open the BBC iPlayer as shown below.

BBC iPlayer

The row of icons on the top right above allow you to search for and download TV programs and save them on the hudl 2. Tap the three dot menu shown on the right to display the above menu, with options to change channels and watch or listen to live TV and radio. Or you can go back and watch or listen to programs broadcast previously, as shown below.

Games

The Google Play Store contains lots of free and inexpensive games in various categories, as shown below.

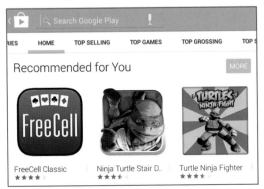

Games apps are installed as apps as discussed on pages 36-39. To launch a game, tap its icon, as shown on the right on the All Apps screen.

Creating a Games Folder

You can group all your games into one folder, as discussed on page 30. Tap the resulting folder icon to open the folder and give it a name. For quick access, the folder icon can be placed on the Favorites Tray by sliding it into a gap created by sliding away another app, as discussed on page 29. In the example below, the **Games** folder has been placed second from the left on the Favorites Tray.

Browsing the Web

Introduction

The Tesco hudl 2 can give you access to millions of Web pages containing the latest high quality information on any subject you care to think of.

The *Google Chrome Web browser* enables you to search the millions of Web pages quickly and easily and displays the results in an attractive and readable format. The *Google search app* is the world's leading Web search program on all platforms – tablet, laptop and desktop computers.

The Tesco hudl 2, which uses the standard Google Android operating system, is an ideal tool for browsing the Internet using Google Chrome. In my opinion this rewarding and useful activity alone justifies the modest purchase price of the hudl 2, not to mention its many other functions such as news, social networking and entertainment, discussed elsewhere in this book.

Some of the main functions of Google Chrome are:

- To search for and display information after entering or speaking *keywords* into the Google search engine.

- To access Web pages after entering their *address* such as **www.babanibooks.com** into the browser.

- To move between Web pages by tapping *links* or *hyperlinks* on a Web page and move forward and backwards between Web pages.

- To *bookmark* Web pages for revisiting at a later time.

Launching Google Chrome

To launch Google Chrome, tap its icon on the All Apps
screen or on the Favorites tray, shown below.

The **Welcome to Google Chrome** screen opens, as shown
below. Tap **Take a tour** to view several pages of notes to help
you get started.

The search bar across the top of the screen is the place to start
your Web browsing activities. Here you enter either the address
of a Web site or *keywords* which should pinpoint the subject you
are interested in.

Entering the Address of a Web Site

Every Web site has a unique address, known as its *URL*, or *Uniform Resource Locator*. A typical Web address is:

www.babanibooks.com.

Type the URL into the search bar, as shown below' and tap the **Go** key on the on-screen keyboard.

For a complicated address you may need to enter the URL in full. However, in practice you'll often find you don't need to be too pedantic; simply entering **babanibooks**, for example, will lead you to the required Web site. If you've visited a site before, it may appear in a list of suggested Web sites which pops up to save you typing the full address.

Instead of typing the URL, as discussed above, you might prefer to tap the microphone icon shown on the right, then speak the Web address.

After entering the address of the Web site into the search bar and pressing **Go**, the Web site's Home Page should quickly open on the screen, as shown in the extract below.

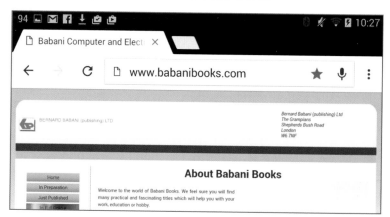

The Keyword Search

This is used to find out about a particular subject rather than visiting a Web site whose address you know, as discussed on the previous page. The World Wide Web seems to contain pages on every conceivable subject. For example, suppose you wanted to find out about the Border Reivers, who were a major part of the turbulent past in the borders between England and Scotland. Simply enter **border reivers** into the Google Chrome search bar, as shown below. (There's no need to use capital letters when entering search criteria — **Border Reivers** or **border reivers** produce the same results).

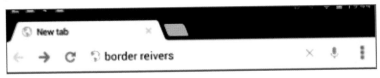

After tapping the **Go** key on the on-screen keyboard, the screen displays a list of Google search results, as shown below.

Only the top search result is shown above in blue but a search often yields millions of results. Google places the most significant results near the top of the list. Some results may be irrelevant to a particular search. For example, historians studying the Border Reivers may not be particularly interested in the Web site of the Border Reivers Rambling Club which might appear in the results.

Each of the blue headings on a search result represents a *link* to a Web page containing the keywords, **Border Reivers** in this example. Tap a link to have a look at the Web site.

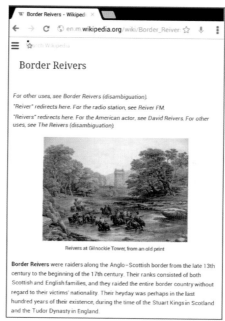

Surfing the Net

On the Web page shown above, some words are highlighted in blue. These are *links* which can be tapped to open further Web pages. Each new page will probably have lots of further links, so tapping these will open a succession of Web pages.

Try typing a few diverse keywords into Google Chrome and see how easy it is to find good information on virtually any subject, no matter how bizarre. Here's a few to get you started:

halebop	histamine	entrevaux
making elderberry wine	samuel johnson	thatching a roof
florence nightingale	hadron collider	shearing a sheep

The Internet is surely the world's largest and most up-to-date encyclopaedia covering almost every known subject. At a more practical level, Google Chrome is probably the DIY enthusiast's best friend. Type any DIY task, such as **mending a puncture**, for example, and numerous Web sites offer helpful advice, often including step-by-step videos.

Previously Visited Pages

As you move between Web pages, you may wish to briefly revisit a page. The back and forward buttons shown on the right and below allow you to quickly move between recently visited pages. Tapping the circular arrow button on the right and below reloads the latest version of a Web page. (For speed, the Chrome browser may load an earlier version of a Web page).

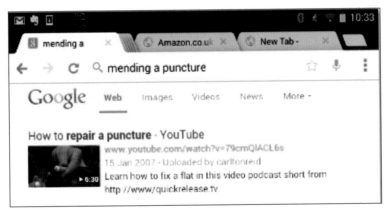

As you move forward or back between Web pages, the keywords from each search, such as **shearing a sheep**, are displayed on the tab at the top left of the screen as shown below.

Tabbed Browsing

When you do a search in Google Chrome and then proceed to surf the Web, as described earlier, there is only one tab displaying the current Web page, as described at the bottom of the previous page. However, Chrome allows you to open each Web page in a tab of their own, so that all the tabs are visible along the top of the screen, as shown in the example below.

This makes it easy to move straight to a particular Web page, rather than moving through them all one at a time using the back and forward buttons. Tap a tab to open that Web page. With a large number of Web pages open, the tabs may be stacked on top of each other and can be moved around by sliding or gently swiping left or right.

Opening a Web Page in Its Own New Tab

Tap the **New tab** icon shown on the right and below.

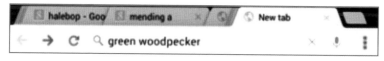

A **New tab** appears, as shown above on the right, with the search bar ready for you to enter your search criteria by typing or speaking. After carrying out the search and selecting a Web page from the results, this page appears on its own tab. The search criteria, in this case **green woodpecker**, appear on the top of the tab, as shown below.

Using the Google App

In the previous examples, Google Chrome was opened by tapping its icon on the Favorites tray. You can also launch Chrome after tapping the Google icon shown on the right, on the All Apps screen. Then enter the search criteria, such as **honey buzzard sightings** in this example, in the Google search bar, as shown below.

Tap on a link in the search results to open a Web page you want to look at. The Web page opens in Google Chrome, in a new tab of its own, **Honey Buzzard...**, in this example, as shown below.

To switch to another Web page from a previous search, simply tap its tab, such as **mending a puncture**, partly shown above.

Closing a Tab

Close a tab by tapping the cross, as shown on the right below.

Bookmarking a Web Page

You can create a series of *bookmarks* so that you can quickly return to your favourite Web pages at any time in the future. With the required Web page open on the screen, tap the star-shaped bookmark icon as shown on the right and on the right of the search bar below.

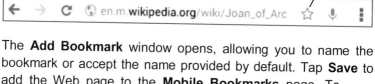

The **Add Bookmark** window opens, allowing you to name the bookmark or accept the name provided by default. Tap **Save** to add the Web page to the **Mobile Bookmarks** page. To view the bookmarks, tap the three dot menu icon shown on the right and then tap **Bookmarks** on the drop-down menu.

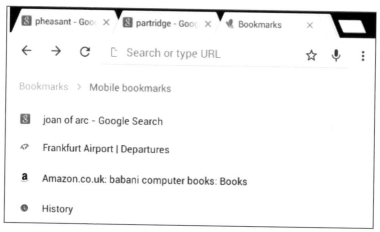

To open one of the bookmarked Web pages, tap its icon on the **Bookmarks** page, as shown above. Press and hold a bookmark icon to display the menu shown on the right, including options to edit and delete a bookmark.

Open in new tab

Open in Incognito tab

Edit bookmark

Delete bookmark

Displaying Your Browsing History

Google Chrome keeps a record, in chronological order, of all the Web pages you've recently visited. Surprisingly there isn't a button to display the History feature. However it can easily be displayed by typing **chrome://history/** into the search bar.

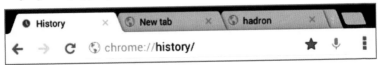

When you tap **Go**, your **History** list is displayed, as shown below.

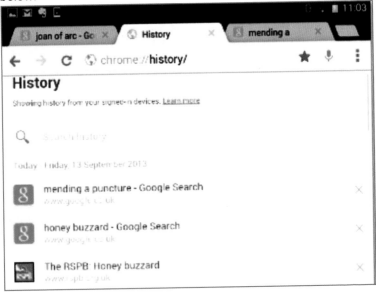

To save time when opening your History, instead of entering **Chrome://history/** into the search bar, create a **History** bookmark, as shown on the right. Creating a bookmark is described on page 87. There are options to **CLEAR BROWSING DATA...** and **Search history**.

Communication and Social Networking

Introduction

This chapter describes the various ways a hudl 2 tablet can be used to communicate with other people. Some of the main apps used for these activities are:

Gmail

Google e-mail used by businesses, friends and families to send messages, documents and photos all over the world.

Skype

Free worldwide *voice* and *video* calls between computers.

Facebook

The most popular *social networking* Web site. Enter your personal *profile* and *timeline* and make *online friends* with people having similar backgrounds and interests.

Twitter

Another very popular social networking site, based on short text messages (*140 characters maximum*) which can be read by anyone who chooses to follow the originator, who may be a celebrity, company or a member of the public.

LinkedIn

This is a special network used by professionals for developing their careers and exploring business opportunities, but is beyond the scope of this book.

Electronic Mail

Gmail is Google's electronic mail service. It's currently the most popular, ahead of other well-known services such as Microsoft's Hotmail and Outlook.com and Yahoo! Mail. Gmail is powerful yet easy to use and very good at filtering out "spam", the unsolicited junk mail or advertising that can waste a lot of your time.

Gmail is used for creating, sending and receiving text messages over the Internet, as an alternative to sending letters by the traditional post. *Replies* can easily be sent to the original sender of a message you've received and, if necessary, to all other recipients of the original message. An e-mail can be *forwarded* to anyone else you think may be interested.

You can maintain an *address book* for all your contacts and *import* into it files of contacts from other e-mail services.

An e-mail message can include photos and documents, known as *attachments,* "clipped" to the message and sent with it.

Gmail is a Web-based e-mail service, so you can access your electronic correspondence from anywhere in the world. All you need is a connection to the Internet and your Gmail username and password, as discussed on page 18. If someone has already used your chosen e-mail address, just add some numbers, such as **stellaaustin86@gmail.com**, to create a unique address.

There are two e-mail apps on the hudl 2 All Apps screen. The yellow **Email** app, shown on the right, is used for accessing any of your other e-mail accounts, such as Hotmail or Outlook.com.

Email

Gmail is opened by tapping its icon, as shown on the right, on the All Apps screen or on the Favorites Tray. When you first start using Gmail, an almost blank screen appears with just the words **No conversations** in the middle. Once you've been using Gmail for a while, there'll be plenty of "conversations", i.e. your messages and the replies.

Gmail

Creating a Message

Tap the **Compose** icon shown on the top right of the screen, as shown on the right and below.

The **Compose** screen opens, as shown below. Enter the main recipient's e-mail address in the **To** bar. Tapping **+CC/BCC** shown on the right below opens two new lines for recipients who will receive either **Carbon Copies** or **Blind Carbon Copies**. The latter don't know who else has received a copy.

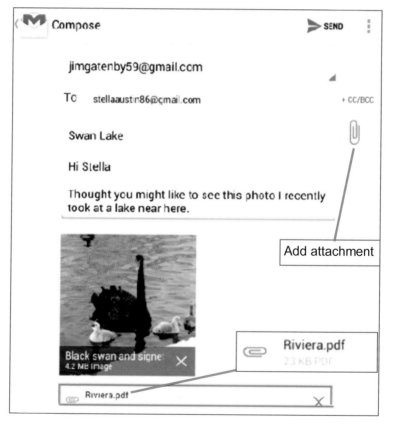

Adding an Attachment

Tap the icon shown on the right and on the previous page. You are then given a choice of locations from which to select the photo, document or some other type of file which you wish to attach to the message. This might be a document saved in My Drive (discussed shortly) or a picture in the Gallery, for example. Tap the required photo, etc., and the attachments should appear on the bottom of the e-mail, as shown on the previous page. The attachments in this example are the swan photo and a PDF document called **Riviera.pdf**.

Sending an E-mail

When all the text has been entered and any attachments added, tap the **SEND** button on the bar across the top of the screen.

Receiving an E-mail

The e-mail will be available for reading by the recipient almost immediately, or as soon as they open their *Inbox*.

The paper clip icon on the right and above indicates that an attachment has been sent. Tap anywhere on the message header above to open the complete message. Tap the small photo to open it fully on the screen. To open an attached document, tap its name, as shown on the right. You are presented with a choice of several apps with which to open the document.

Skype

This is a service which allows you to make free *voice* and *video* calls all over the world. Calls between two computers are absolutely free. If you use your tablet to call a mobile phone or landline there is a charge, for which you need a Skype account with some credit in it.

Hundreds of millions of people use Skype to make voice and video calls. You can also send photographs and instant text messages or make and send a video. hudl 2 tablets are fully equipped for Skype, with a front-facing webcam and built in microphone and speakers. If you also have a rear-facing camera, this can be used to show views of your surroundings during a video call. The Skype app in the Google Play Store is free and can be installed as described in Chapter 3.

Start Skype by tapping its icon on the All Apps screen, as shown on the right. Then sign in using an existing Skype username and password or a Microsoft account. Alternatively, if necessary, create a new Skype account. When you sign in, contacts from your address book are displayed, as shown below.

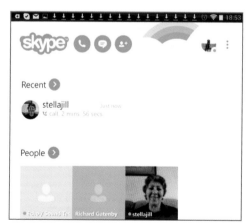

The Opening Skype Screen

Making a Skype Call

Any contacts currently online are displayed with a green dot, as shown on the right and at the bottom of the previous page.

Tap the name or thumbnail of a contact who is currently online. The following icons are available when making a Skype call:

 Start a voice only call

 Start a video call

 Record and then send a video

When you call a contact, their photo and name appear on the screen. The functions of the icons are listed on the next page.

Making a Skype call

Receiving a Skype Call

When someone "Skypes" you, the tablet will emit a distinctive ring and the caller's name appears on the screen. Tap the green phone icon shown on the left below to answer the call.

| Receiving a call | Answering a call |

Shown below are the main icons used when answering calls:

     Answer a video or voice call

     Switch video on or off

     Switch microphone on or off

    Show dialling pad and messages

    End or reject a call

Facebook

Facebook is the biggest social network, with over a billion users all over the world. To join Facebook, you must be aged over 13 years and have a valid e-mail address. You can access Facebook on a hudl 2 using the Android Facebook app, installed from the Play Store, as discussed in Chapter 3. You also need to *sign up* for a Facebook account and in future *sign in* with your e-mail address and password.

First you create your own *Profile* in the form of a *Timeline*, as shown on the right. This can include personal details such as your schools, employers and hobbies and interests. Facebook then provides lists of people with similar interests to yourself, who you may want to invite to be one of your Facebook *friends*. Anyone who accepts will be able to exchange news, information, photos and videos with you.

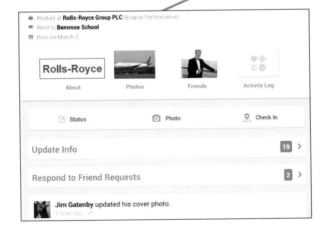

Facebook Security and Privacy

The *audience selector* shown on the right appears 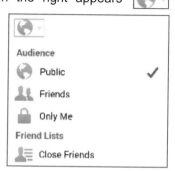 against the items of personal information in your profile. Tapping the audience selector icon displays a drop-down menu, as shown on the right, enabling you to set the level of privacy for each item, ranging from **Public** to **Only me**. **Public** means *everyone* can see the information, including people you don't know.

Status Updates

These are used to post your latest information and news and usually consist of a short text message and probably one or more photos. Tap **Status** on the centre left of the Facebook screen shown on the previous page to open the **Write Post** window shown below. Tap **To:** to select the audience. Then enter the text of your post, replacing **What's on your mind?** shown below.

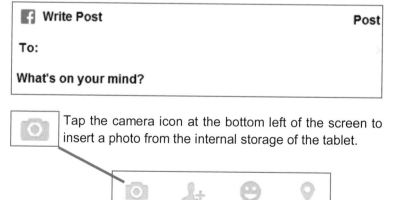

Tap the camera icon at the bottom left of the screen to insert a photo from the internal storage of the tablet.

Finally tap **Post**, shown on the right above and your friends will receive the update in their *News Feed*.

Twitter

Like Facebook, Twitter is a social networking Web site used by hundreds of millions of people. There is a free app for Twitter in the Google Play Store. The app can be installed on the hudl 2 as discussed in Chapter 3. Signing up to Twitter is free. Once signed up you can either use your e-mail address and password to sign in or you can enter your Twitter username such as **@jimsmith**. Some of the main features of Twitter are:

- Twitter is a Web site used for posting text messages, known as *tweets*, of up to 140 characters in length.

- You can include a 160 character *personal profile* on your Twitter page.

- Photographs can be posted with a tweet.

- Twitter is based on people *following*, i.e. reading the tweets of other people, such as celebrities, politicians and companies marketing their products or services.

- You can follow anyone you like, but you can't choose who follows you. If you have no followers, anything you post on Twitter will remain unread. You could encourage your friends and family to follow you and each other on Twitter, to share your latest news.

- *Hashtags*, such as *#climatechange*, for example, make it simple for other people to find all the tweets on a particular subject. The hashtag is included within a tweet. Tapping the hashtag displays all the tweets on that subject, which might be a campaign or a debate.

- If you like a tweet, it can be *retweeted* to all of your followers, together with comments of your own.

- You can send *replies* to a tweet.

Sending a Tweet

Tap **What's happening?** at the bottom left of the Home screen and then replace these words with your own message.

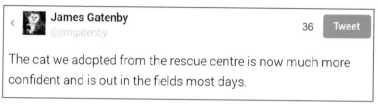

The number **36** at the top right above is the number of characters still available out of the maximum of 140 allowed in a tweet.

Two icons appear at the bottom of the **Tweet** window, as shown below. Tapping the left-hand icon uses the hudl 2's GPS to pinpoint your location and include this as a note in the Tweet.

Tapping the right-hand icon above displays the two icons shown on the right. The camera icon is used to take photos with either of the hudl 2's built-in cameras. The right-hand icon is used to select a photo already saved on the hudl

2. The picture is then included in the tweet. When the tweet is finished, tap **Tweet** shown at the top right of this page.

Your followers will see your tweet in their Home screen, as shown on the next page.

From the three button menu at the top right of the screen, tap **Settings** and **General**. Tap to tick the box next to **Image previews** to display photos in a tweet. If the box is not ticked, a blue text link is displayed instead, as discussed on the next page.

Responding to a Tweet

If the reader taps a tweet, the following toolbar is displayed.

These icons enable you to respond to a tweet in various ways. Reading from left to right, they are:

Reply, **Retweet**, mark as **Favorite** and **Share** with other people.

Viewing Photographs

As discussed on the previous page, depending on the **Settings**, instead of a photo, the reader of a tweet may see a blue link embedded in the text, such as **pic.twitter.com/g43TrgzchM** shown below. This link is created by Twitter automatically .

 James Gatenby @jimgatenby   17m
The cat we adopted from the rescue centre is now much more confident and is out in the fields most days. pic.twitter.com/
g43TrgzchM

Tap the tweet as shown above to open the photo on the screen.

Working With Photos

Introduction

The Tesco hudl 2 is an ideal platform for taking, viewing and sharing photographs and videos.

The hudl 2 has a slot for a Micro SD card which can also be used in a standard digital camera, simplifying the process of transferring photos and videos to the hudl 2. These are then readily available for viewing on the hudl 2 at any time. The photos can also be shared in e-mails or in any posts you put on social networks such as Facebook and Twitter, as discussed earlier in this book.

Some of the main methods of putting photos and videos on the hudl 2 are:

- Taking a photo (or making a video) with one of the hudl 2's two built-in cameras.

- Copying photos onto the hudl 2 from a separate digital camera or an SD card, Micro SD card or flash drive.

- Copying photos from a smartphone to the hudl 2 using a *Bluetooth* wireless connection.

- Copying photos that have been stored on a laptop or desktop computer, as discussed in Chapter 9.

- Downloading photos using Facebook, Twitter or e-mail, as discussed in Chapter 7

- Copying or *syncing* photos to the hudl 2 from other computers of various types using cloud storage systems such as *Google Drive* and *Dropbox*, as discussed in Chapter 9.

Using the hudl 2's Built-in Cameras

The hudl 2 has two cameras:

- A 1.2MP (megapixel) camera on the front of the hudl 2 for use in video calls using Skype and for taking 'selfies'.

- A 5MP camera on the back of the hudl 2 for taking general photographs and making videos.

Tap the camera icon shown on the right, on the Apps screen. It will probably launch the rear camera ready for you to take an ordinary photograph. To make a video call, when using Skype for example, the front camera launches automatically showing your face, etc. This front camera can also be used to take a 'selfie' for inclusion in a Facebook or Twitter update.

Switching Between Front and Rear Cameras

Tap the **Camera** app shown above then tap the small 3 dot menu button shown on the right. Then tap the lower icon shown on the right and below to switch between front and rear cameras.

Selecting Photo or Video Mode

Swipe in from the left and tap either **Camera** or **Video** from the menu on the left of the screen, shown here on the right.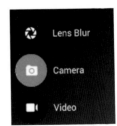

Taking a Photo

Select **Camera** as shown on the previous page at the bottom right. Then tap the black and white Camera icon, shown here on the right, to take a photo with the selected camera. You will hear a noise as the photo is taken.

Making a Video

Select **Video** as shown on the previous page at the bottom right. Then tap the video camera icon shown on the right to start recording. Tap the square icon shown on the right to end the recording.

Viewing Photos and Videos

Photos and videos taken with the hudl 2 can now be viewed after tapping the **Gallery** icon, shown on the right and then selecting the **Camera** Album.

Tap to open a photo, then tap the menu button shown on the right. This displays options including **Delete**, **Slideshow**, **Crop**, **Rotate** and **Edit** the photo.

Capturing a Screenshot

To capture a copy of the screen, simultaneously hold down the **Power** button and the **Volume** button (at the volume down end). The screenshot can then be viewed in the **Screenshots** album in the **Gallery** or sent using the sharing button shown below on the right. Shown on the right is a screenshot, as used in this book, of the hudl 2 All Apps screen.

The *sharing* button shown on the right often appears and can be used to send a photo to Photos, Dropbox, Google Drive, e-mail, Facebook and Twitter, etc.

Using the hudl 2's Micro SD Card Slot

Unlike some tablets, the Tesco hudl 2 has a slot, as shown on page 14, into which you can insert a Micro SD card of up to 32GB. This can be used to increase the storage on the hudl 2 from the basic 16GB up to 48GB.

Importing Photos from a Micro SD Card

The Micro SD card can also be used as a camera card to simplify the viewing and importing of photos to the hudl 2. An adapter, shown on the right, the size of a standard SD card, enables the Micro SD card to be used in a normal digital camera. Then the Micro SD card, complete with photos, can be removed from the

Adapter

Micro SD Card

adapter and inserted into the Micro SD slot in the hudl 2.

Tap the **Gallery** icon shown on the right. After a short time the new photos show up in an **Album** in the Gallery. Tap on the album to display the photos in **Grid view** and then tap a photo to display it full screen.

Gallery

Tap the full size image to display the menu and sharing buttons shown on the right. As discussed on the previous page, these allow you to manage and edit the photos and send them to various destinations such as Photos, Google Drive, Dropbox, Twitter and Facebook.

Images stored by the Photos app or in Dropbox or Google Drive can be viewed after tapping the icons shown below. Google Drive and Dropbox are discussed in detail in Chapter 9.

Photos

Dropbox

Drive

Using the hudl 2's Micro USB Port

The *Micro USB* port built into the hudl 2 and shown on page 14 can easily be converted to a full-size standard USB port using an OTG (On The Go) cable, as shown below.

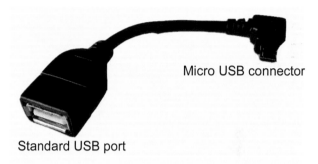

Micro USB connector

Standard USB port

An OTG cable

The OTG cable can be used for connecting the following USB devices to a tablet, for the copying of photos and other files.

- A separate digital camera.
- A USB card reader with standard SD card.
- A USB flash drive/memory stick.

Apps are available to carry out the actual *importing* or copying of the photos to the hudl 2, as discussed shortly.

Connecting a Digital Camera

Digital cameras are normally provided with a cable which has a USB connector or plug. This is used for charging the camera's battery and can also be used for copying photos to the hudl 2. Insert the OTG cable into the Micro USB port on the hudl 2. Insert the USB connector on the camera cable into the standard USB port on the OTG cable. Then connect the other end of the cable to the camera. The hudl 2 should detect the camera and you can then import the photos, as discussed shortly.

Connecting an SD Card Using a Card Reader

This is used to import photos from a full-size, standard SD card. USB card readers are available, as shown on the right, which plug directly into the standard USB port on the OTG cable shown on the previous page. Some USB card readers have several slots to accommodate different types of SD card.

USB card reader with full size SD card inserted

Connecting a USB Flash Drive

Photos stored on a *USB flash drive* (or *memory stick*) can be imported into a tablet after inserting the flash drive into the USB port on an OTG cable, shown on the previous page.

USB connector or plug

USB flash drive

Transferring Photos from a USB Device.

Apps are available in the Google Play Store, such as the Nexus Media Importer, which can be used with the hudl 2 to import photos from a USB device such as a camera, SD card reader or flash drive, etc.

Nexus Media Importer

The Nexus Media Importer opens and you can select **Folders** or **All Photos**. A small sample from **All Photos** is shown on the right. Tap on a photo, such as **Boxter.JPG** to open it as shown on the top of the next page

Photos
Nexus Media Importer

All Photos

Root

Atlantic Bridge.JPG

Boxter.JPG

The Nexus Media Importer

The row of icons shown above appear at the top right of the Nexus Media Importer screen and have the following functions:

 Saves a **Copy** of the selected photo in the **Pictures** album in the **Gallery** in the Internal Storage of the tablet.

 The **Move** button *transfers* a photo to the **Pictures** folder.

 The Delete button removes photos from a USB storage medium such as an SD card.

 Use the **Share** button to send copies of photos to e-mail, Facebook, Twitter and Dropbox, etc.

 The **Menu** button has options including **Edit**, **Slide Show** and **Rotate**.

Google+ Auto-Backup

This backs up all your photos and videos to the Photos section of Google+. Tap the icon shown on the right to view all your photos. To check **Auto-Backup** is **ON**, tap the **Photos** icon, then tap the three button menu icon shown above on the left. Finally tap **Settings** then **Auto-Backup**. To view the backed up photos, type **#autobackup** in the search bar of the Photos app.

Copying Photos from a Smartphone

This can be done using the *Bluetooth* wireless technology built into the phone and the hudl 2. The general method is as follows:

Pairing the hudl 2 and a Smartphone

- In **Settings** on both devices, make sure Bluetooth is **ON** and each device is set as **Discoverable** or **Visible to all Bluetooth devices nearby**.
- On the hudl 2, tap **SEARCH FOR DEVICES**.
- Confirm that the same **PIN** number appears on both devices.
- The two devices are now *paired* i.e. connected wirelessly, as shown below.

Transferring a Photo from the Smartphone to the hudl 2

- Open the photo full-size on the smartphone.
- From the phone menu, select **Send** then **Bluetooth**.
- On the phone select **hudl 2** under **Select Device.**
- The file transfer starts.
- On the hudl 2, swipe down from the top left **Notification Area** and tap **Do you want to receive this file?** and then tap **Accept** under **Accept the file?**
- The file transfer is completed and the file can now be viewed in the Gallery on the hudl 2.

Cloud Computing and File Management

Introduction

Cloud computing is the storage of *files* such as photos and documents on powerful Internet computers known as *servers*. The servers are provided and managed by large companies such as Google and Dropbox. Storing many of your files in the clouds means you don't need bulky hard disc drives inside computers. This has contributed to the development of very small hand-held tablets like the hudl 2, which can be just as powerful as much larger computers.

The general method is that you have a cloud storage app such as Google Drive or Dropbox. Dropbox provides up to 2GB of free storage space while more is available for a monthly fee. Google offers 15GB of free storage for Drive, Gmail and Google+ Photos. Apps for Dropbox and Drive can be downloaded from the Play Store if not already installed on the hudl 2. The Dropbox or Google Drive app is set up on each computer and you access it with a username and password.

When you save a file in, say, Dropbox, on one computer, it's automatically copied to the clouds and *synced* to all your other machines. For example, I use a desktop computer for typesetting the chapters of books such as this one. By saving each chapter in Dropbox on my desktop computer it's automatically synced to my other computers, including the hudl 2. The hudl 2 can open the chapters, which are saved as PDF (Portable Document Format) files. So I can read through and check the chapters anywhere and at any time on the hudl 2 or any other computer.

Accessing Files in the Clouds

The very popular cloud storage apps, Dropbox and Google Drive are shown below in the Play Store. These may be already on your hudl 2 but, if not, they can be freely downloaded from the Play Store and installed as described in Chapter 3.

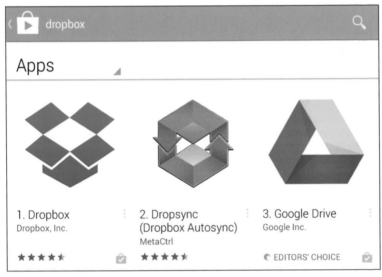

Dropbox

After you install Dropbox, create an account on the hudl 2 by signing up with your e-mail address and password. If you have other computers such as a laptop or a desktop you can sign up to Dropbox on them after opening the website at:

www.dropbox.com

On a Windows PC machine this will place a **Dropbox** folder on the Windows/File Explorer, as shown on the right. Any files you save in the Dropbox folder will be synced to the Dropbox on your other computers such as the hudl 2.

Similarly photos and other files saved on the hudl 2 can be transferred to your other computers using the share icon on the hudl 2, shown on the right. This appears after opening the photo on the full screen and tapping it, as discussed on pages 103 and 104.

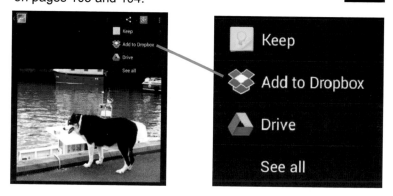

Tap **Add to Dropbox** shown above to copy the file to Dropbox (Or tap **Drive** shown above to send it to Google Drive, discussed on the next page). Files saved in Dropbox (and also in Google Drive) have several advantages:

- Files can be viewed on any computer connected to the Internet anywhere, once you've signed in to Dropbox.
- All computers have the same, latest versions of files.
- The files are professionally backed up and managed on the host server computers in the "clouds".

One risk is that if you accidentally delete a file on one machine, it will no longer be available on any of your other computers.

Cloud storage systems like Dropbox and Google Drive are extremely useful and efficient. However, it's also a good idea to make backup copies of important files on a separate storage medium such as a flash drive/memory stick.

Google Drive

The hudl 2 is controlled by the Google Android operating system and *Drive* is Google's popular cloud storage system. Drive can be used with the hudl 2 and, if necessary, installed from the Play Store, as described in Chapter 3.

Google Drive works in a very similar way to **Dropbox**, just described. You install the app on the hudl 2 with a Gmail address and a password. The method of uploading files to **Drive** on the hudl 2 is the same as sharing files to **Dropbox**, as discussed on page 111.

On any other computers which you may use, install the app or, on laptop and desktop PCs, install a **Google Drive** folder, after visiting the website at drive.google.com. Next tap **Install Drive for your computer**. Repeat this for all the computers you wish to automatically sync files to.

Any files you share with **Drive** on the hudl 2, will appear in **Drive** on all your other computers. Similarly, if you drag and drop files to the **Google Drive** folder on a laptop or desktop PC, as shown on the right, these files will automatically be synced to **My Drive** on the hudl 2, as shown below. To display **My Drive** on the hudl 2, tap the **Drive** icon shown at the top right of this page.

Google Docs

Once you've installed Google Drive you immediately have access to *Google Docs*, which is a suite of free *web-based software* and includes word processing and spreadsheet apps. This software is available on any computer with Google Drive installed, after you've signed in with your Gmail username and password.

Tap the **Drive** icon shown on the right to open **My Drive**, shown at the bottom of the previous page. Then tap the **Create** icon at the bottom of the **My Drive** screen, as shown below.

A menu is displayed with options to create a word processing document or a spreadsheet. The spreadsheet and word processing apps in Google Docs have all the usual features needed to produce substantial documents.

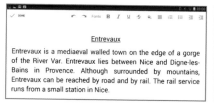

Word processing in Google Docs   Spreadsheet in Google Docs

When you finish work, tap **Done** and the document is automatically saved in Google Drive in the clouds and synced to any other computers on which you have installed Google Drive.

As discussed elsewhere in this book, you can connect the hudl 2 to a Bluetooth keyboard and HDMI TV or monitor, if necessary.

Making Files Available Offline

You may want to look at photos and other files offline, where you have no Wi-Fi or Internet connection. You can check a file for offline access by turning Wi-Fi **OFF**, as discussed on page 15, then trying to open the file.

Offline Access in Dropbox

Open the listing of files and photos in Dropbox then tap the circled down arrow and tap the **Favorite** star to make the file viewable offline. Alternatively open the file on the screen and tap the **Favorite** star.

Offline Access in Google Drive

Open the file or file listing in Drive and tap the information icon shown on the right. Then make sure **Keep on device** is switched **ON** as shown below.

Keep on device   ON

File Management Using a PC

Android tablets like the hudl 2 don't have a built-in *file manager* app to carry out tasks such as copying, moving, deleting and renaming files. However, you can use a laptop or desktop PC computer to manage the files on a hudl 2. Connect the hudl 2 to a USB port on the laptop or desktop machine, using the cable normally used to charge the hudl 2's battery. I used this method to transfer screenshots from the hudl 2 to my PC

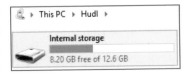

machine for inclusion in this book. The hudl 2 appears in the File Explorer or Windows Explorer on the PC just like an external disc drive or flash drive, etc. Files and folders on the hudl 2 can be moved around the hudl 2 or copied to and from the PC using **Cut**, **Copy**, **Paste** and managed using **Delete**, etc.

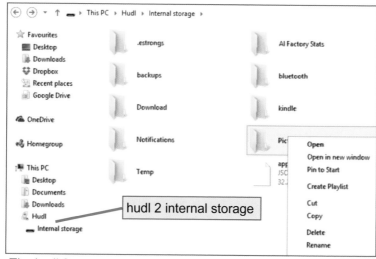

The hudl 2 connected to a PC, shown in Windows File Explorer

File Manager Apps

Several free file manager apps are available for downloading and installing from the Play Store, as discussed in Chapter 3. These include ES File Explorer and File Manager.

If you import files from a PC into a hudl 2, such as those in the popular Word or Excel formats, etc., the hudl 2 on its own will not be able to open them. However, free apps in the Play Store such as WPS Office (also known as Kingsoft Office) can open, edit

and create documents in a variety of popular formats such as .doc, .docx, .txt,.pdf, .xls,.xlsx and .csv.

Cloud Printing from the hudl 2

Google Cloud Print is a free app used for printing from a tablet like the hudl 2 and installed from the Play Store as described in Chapter 3.

If you have a printer connected to a laptop or desktop PC, this is referred to as a *Classic* printer and needs to be set up in the Google Chrome Web browser as described below. (A *Cloud Ready* wireless printer connects to the Web without being attached to a computer. This shouldn't need any setting up).

For setting up, a classic printer is attached to a laptop or desktop computer which has Chrome installed. Open Chrome on the PC and make sure you're signed in with your Gmail address and password. Open the Chrome menu by tapping or clicking the icon shown on the right.

From the menu, select **Settings** and then scroll down the screen and at the bottom select Show advanced settings. Scroll down the next screen and under **Google Cloud Print** select **Manage** and then **Add printers**. Select the printer you wish to use, as shown below. Then tap **Add printer** to complete the process.

Tap and hold a document or photo in Google Drive then select **Print** from the menu. Then select your printer and tap the **Print** button. In the hudl 2 Gallery use the share icon and **See all** shown on page 111 to send a photo to **Cloud Print** then select your printer and tap **Print**.

Index